ABOUT THE AUTHOR

Sam J. Grudgings is a poet perpetually on the edge of collapse, shortlisted for the Outspoken Prize 2020 & longlisted in 2019. Renowned for his off-kilter, frenetic delivery & boundary pushing stage dynamic, Sam grew up in the punk scene & it shows.

Injecting gallows humour into fiercely wrought metaphors, Sam subverts the narratives of addiction, bringing a wry touch to devastating subjects whilst still allowing himself the space to be painfully candid & devastatingly vulnerable. He yells stories about recovery, mental illness, loss, fighting god & cities made of teeth because it's cheaper than therapy & is less physically taxing than pornography

Sam runs workshops on performance as well as campaigning for the recognition of lived experience in professional & academic circles. He endeavours to bring poetry to everyone eventually. He can be found if you know where to look.

https://www.samjgrudgings.co.uk
Twitter: @storygiverpoet
Instagram: @samjgrudgings

The
Bible

II

Sam J. Grudgings

"I want to create a myth that I can one day become."
David Wojnarowicz

VERVE
POETRY PRESS
BIRMINGHAM

PUBLISHED BY VERVE POETRY PRESS
https://vervepoetrypress.com
mail@vervepoetrypress.com

FIRST PUBLISHED NOV 2021

Printed and bound in the UK
by ImprintDigital, Exeter

978-1-912565-69-6

*This book would not be possible without the patience of
Myriam San Marco.*

*However, dead friends take precedence
so this book is dedicated instead to
Meryl & Leon*

*Wish you could have read this one lads,
I reckon you would have loved it.*

CONTENTS

Behemoth

OLD TESTAMENT

NEW TESTAMENT

THE PHARISEES, THE PROPHETS, THE UNBURDEN, THE RECANTATION

The

Bible

II

Behemoth *(/bɪˈhiːməθ, ˈbiːə-/; Hebrew: בהמות, behemot)*

1. THROUGH THE SOFT WINDSHIELD I REMAKE MY ENTRANCE TO THE WORLD. I orphan the stomach denied entry to its contents, no longer a father to the open inside me. In the house of fire I chose to live, to accept my empty never made me. Never caused me or the devastation or the empire of want & ruin or the endless, endless need. Thirty years & a body has yet to be made worth saving. I barely grew up in the scar left behind. Shrapnel halo, throat of void, just one more handful of napalm. Holy wake up call, father rebreather. Decerebrate me. If offered clemency, I will take my railway spine &, knowing kneeling never hurt at the scenes of accidents, I will ask the mountain if it will not come with us just this once.

2. REBALANCING THE STORY ECONOMY. If you hold a gun to the head of an addict the barrell will transform into birdsong. Falling to your knees in despair only looks like prayer because there is no other acceptable form of beseeching yourself for change. Look at yourself motherfucker & say you do not recognise the monsters. We all lie to feel good about ourselves. We all want to push our hands through a body denied a purpose, to give ourselves to a god that does not want & still be able to call it a sacrifice because it is the cause that matters. Harbour the missing weeks & the days we can't get rid of. Retell ourselves the regurgitative strategy of the fervent, those still stuck praying who will find out they are better off atheists for all the good it will do. God calls me derelict & I force myself to swallow.

3. THE AFTERTHOUGHT OF AN EVENING DEMANDS THE MOST CALLOUS THINGS OF YOU. You must confess all the things you are - all the bodies in the lake & the man sank with chicken wire; confess that every hole in your body is an informant; confess that you do not know how you survived you just did. Remember all the almost waking up in morgues, forgetting the night before. Waking up to another morning of roses & razor blades & piss & shame. When I was alive I had no idea a torso could hold so much water. This means I am immortal in last minute installments. The longest decade of the ten shortest years, my favourite longest lasting metamorphosis. A decade of god calling & me only answering in the negative. The unfounded thing that runs through my head is that this internal monologue might be a messiah complex. But then the difference between revisionism & recidivism is improvisation. This is a resurrection waiting to happen - the hard part is the waiting.

4. SELF PORTRAIT AS ADDICT SELLING SELF PORTRAITS OF SELF AS ADDICT TO GET BY So. Those of us singing death songs for the nostalgic; us - deported for wearing our cauls as litmus paper, us - with all these flesh songs, god rhetoric & guts decanted from the vestibule of our unholy past must negotiate the conditions of our release. Plead we were just kids doing our impression of what we thought adulthood would be. I don't blame myself for becoming the abyss, I do take responsibility for those who took the deep of me. Take responsibility for those my maelstrom heart trapped. Take responsibility for the cadaver they're trying to rehabilitate through autopsy. If you want me to wake you must raise my whalefall skin, teach me less to walk on water & more accept it, you must put my fathom body back together. To show the biology of my contrition, to begin the work of regifting my flotsam self to the congregation. Work through the opt out policy of donating phantom limbs, find out just how holy we are. I can only speak of the slow it took in learning addicts are aspects of god trying to understand mortality by dying. There is no midnight after feeding - anything less than god is human. God calls - an endless loop of demand. I acknowledge only voicemails' deluge - acknowledge only that martyrdom requires evidence that the penitent have suffered.

5. ROAD AS AUTHOR PROXY God calls but I will not answer. God calls - his need the horizon. God calls but this is not the time for redemption but for peeling myself raw from the asphalt. For waking from the chest cavity of all I held dear to me, harbouring my museum skin of ten years of needing & curating a new continent of myself to explore. I will pick idly at all that's left of my roadkill & highway remains. The strata of my rib cage depicts a dead god. All fossil deposits & bodies of who we were. My asphalt mouth will drown all incoming traffic. Somehow become the road of history rather than it's remnants. I will archive every loss & catalogue it. I will surrender to the one gift we try to deny ourselves. Tomorrow. Tomorrow. Tomorrow. Give us this day, this daily offering of our being & we will learn what to do with it. Innovate this exhibition of being human. Of living well. Of living enough. Of simply living. Trying to escape all the condemnation our bodies wrought on our past. I'm accepting drive-thru skin grafts. I'm accepting any journey that takes me away. I am accepting that healing is a process that must not be interrupted.

OLD TESTAMENT

stained glass ethics experiment

I know escape

drinking blood, every vessel is stained glass.

Worship long enough & there are windows
in everyone, I make exits out of people.

If I make it to the solace of my knees I wonder
how penitence became a sanctuary,

how the desperate sermons delivered on falling
stem from my rock bottom reverence of heights,

how fortunate I have been to survive.

Nothing drowns you if you swallow
oceans. I know salt water is a baptism

in desecrated beds. I had to decide
to sink beneath the fracture

of the illustrated window of the ocean
or recover my breathing. Apostate of

the undertow pick a more subtle monster than martyrdom

god fragment I : Jehovah's wetness

I am broken by the people
I see myself reflected in.
I shed bridges like skin to keep
seven years of an echo between us knowing
burning is overrated,

breathe in the wet cement
you carved your name into.
Precious emergency, if I had been better
designed, my failures would be by committee.
The obdurate of my throat

has banned worship,
cellos in place of lungs
& petals of flesh coughed into a handshake.
Survival
is a better story than success.

Paranoia Theology

(after China Mieville)

1. For excommunicated prophets to bottle gods the necessity of rituals is forgotten. Intervention is bureaucracy not kindness. If comfort is needed, their church has always maintained the morning was a false prophecy. If they get it right just once they will be absolved of ever needing to get it right again.

2. Canonizing the last standing for their least proud moments. Retconning the reformationist principles of accidents. Harbouring molars in the crooks of arms holding each other close. All of these are ways of acknowledging your failures without recalibrating. Telling your worshippers you are no longerworthy of their prayers but in need of them is a rejection of the demands made of yourself. Do not believe in the prophecy of empties held to ears to commune with past lives, only in tactile gods. You have to really feel the pain of sacrament for miracles to mean anything.

3. There was a man whose body was a radio with them once. Body as a conduitfor prayer. Body as a conduit for a form of hope that's easy to sing along to. Body as the martyrdom of celebratory movements. When they dismantled him for the secrets of his broadcast they applauded their bloody handiwork too readily. This serves the purpose of reminding them whatever side of the battle they fall on, retribution is simply a point of view.

4. Everything is fit to be worshipped. By choosing their own inadequacies they became addicts of collapse & history & never questioned what they were really praying to. There are ways to become experts on cults. One is to be worshipped. The other is to give in.

Requiem For Open & Abandoned Spaces

The Wisest Man built his house with sand, so nothing lasted & no one ever mattered.

& you, knowing god as well you do, respond that permanence is a state of mind, say nothing is concrete but can never find a way to make this lasting matter. There are blueprints for abandoned places inside us all. With fingerprints immortalised in architecture, me & the orphanage bodied have been ransacking churches hoping to find more holy. Tell ourselves it's a problem language that makes you doubt the wound. Tell ourselves not to balk at the distance of who we were. Believe if the tender skyline of a city vanished the night would be responsible. This concrete purgatory. This five & a half minutes of dismantling myself to reveal the raw empty bone hallway of leaving. Find things among me that make it seem like there is no echo here - across the alley, at the condemned hospital, they pumped our stomachs for words. Found sounds we had forgotten. Found municipal disinvestment & everyone left behind. Found an orrery of birds. They replaced the prophecies with charcoal & told us now is not a good time to misrepresent ourselves. Thinking they were helping, they built empty houses within us for our bodies to launder the inerrancy of their doctrine. I demolish my expectations. I reserve the right to be wrong about god. My skin shifts westward & I am made of impossible monsters. Any moment now, the mistake of asking will fall out of my mouth; was I good enough?

Did I prevent enough? Was unwriting me from your history enough? You will respond in kind - that time cannot be directly perceived - must be reconstructed by the brain, inferred by our senses – we trust that all this will last so it does. The horror of what we would return to if we were not cautious. There is a parasitic choir in my angel head. They are all a version of me I did my best to forget. Against my better judgement I must sit with all those left behind, welcome them into the deep empty & let them remind me of everything I have ever done. In being petitioned by my past lives I tell them I am not a democracy & they tell me that's precisely what the problem is.

I   tell   them
collapse   is

tell them

tell   them   I

collapse   is

collapse   is   .   I

collapse

I tell   them   welcome

tell   them   I   am   a   holy   city   devoid   of   occupants.   Fragmented

narratives of seeking. A better life elsewhere. If I could be anywhere else but me

I would. They tell me the suburbs of my past are gentrified by nostalgia & you agree.

Collapse. Collapse. Collapse. I am pretending things are better than they are again.

I take pains to remember our yielding to the towering architecture of a mutual ribcage.

You respond in kind by turning your shoulders into planning permission. Flesh of city,

Church of empty. Cathedral of you. I have tried to document each step I took, every

trespass that needs to be forgiven. I have held my distance, the autopsy of my past, the

diplomacy of making amends. But you still insist the law of trespass says the burden is

on the intrepid - if you have looked then you are guilty by association of finding. I

concede to the urbanization of my outer reaches. The architecture of gore & spleen,

the runes of our blueprint bones. I am so familiar with the surgical reality of my own

mortal matter I can recite its demolition songs. I unburden my body of unnecessary

meat, make way for the fresh development of an unwieldy architect. You say to leave

the vivisection for those least qualified. To pore over my necessary. To eulogize the

collapse & forget the man. Make me Saint of nothing. Make me Saint of Cassandra.

Make me Saint of empty cities.The problem with perspective is you look in mirrors &

see men wearing the houses they used to be. The problem with nostalgia is you never

know if the echoing voices are coming from far away or just repeating themselves.

The   problem   with   prophecy   is   -   it   is   so   easy   to   get   it   wrong.

This is how angels make themselves known
(translation of a text received from a friend)

You[1] need [2] to stop [3] drinking.[4]

---

[1] I hope for everyone's sake I haven't happened to anyone else. We still never talk sometimes. Sometimes. Sometimes shadows, fragile & callous, erupt unwanted from my spine & my silhouette remains untrustable. I doubt the absence of my light. I resent my shadow for it's impermanence. For what it's worth, I wouldn't miss me either.

[2] All I know is need. I used to have rituals for the loss of sleep. I used to have monuments to my demand. Stiff upper lips plagued with white knuckles, a body plagued by portals. How beautiful my lost looks hidden in regret. How mysterious my empty looks in salvation rhetoric & hindsight.

[3] Fists clenched into stomachs to quell the sickening, the rising gorge of your anger made physical in bile, if you tuck your thumb into a punch it settles the gag reflex & breaks the bone. We call this a compromise. I've found myself referring to myself as a compromise. Referring to myself, third person, is a compromise that I am not who I was. Referring to myself third person, past tense after all is a compromise. After all, after all the other people I might have been, I have finally decided to be present.

[4] Author proxy as bloated corpse as plot device. We found ourselves in the quarry & became the body, a technique that manifests the reader. We found ourselves poking at the deus ex machina, dead by Chekhov's gun, & became the corpse we had discovered. A narrative function to make the audience complicit. We found ourselves & became both the refusal to answer the call & the atonement with the abyss. In lieu of anything better to become I became better.

[5] I have no idea what he meant.

how saviour complexes damage the salvaged

a contrapuntal

SINK

Absolution doesn't exist.

                    can't rectify problems it tries to determine

January is an oxbow lake;

                    in the end an autopsy by any other name

is an exhibit parents dredge history from;

                    things they claimed they pulled from me

bezoars; typewriter keys; more lakes &

                    my ribcage, I only remember

empty spaces; the words maybe tomorrow;

                    I've yet to see the evidence of

a parliament of angels crowing judgement

                    I'm not listening to god's opinion about me

my pockets leaden with excuses so

                    I'm scared I must hate my own.

waters' sneer will close above my disorder

                    I've worn so many good faces for living

I ache into the violence of forgetfulness

                    to salvage the taste of survival,

I envy last words,

                    to make it to land

to be healed of a body's need for touch

                    if we make it through this I promise

to be succinct & finite as the ocean's wish.

                    said the drowning to the shore

                    SURFACE

Yellow livers in the hostile architecture of our bodies nostalgia

What made you want to be careful
      i) what you wished for?
      ii) is it this?
      iii) iconoclastics diagnoses.

Crabbed hands holy. Doctors' scrawl illegible:
      take two *you should have*
      called us sooner, there is not
      much we can do now

The glory of deciding, knowing revelation is a choice
camera obscuras the shadow of palms against penance faces.
      i) We wear prayers as expressions in these rooms.
      ii) The roof's purpose is opaque so leave

to work on your breathing, humble in the misstep of your throat, find yourself
      i) penitent beneath
      ii) the awkwardness of evening.

There's some elegant design, prosaic in indignance.
Loose limbed compurgator
      i) on the trade off of favours,
      ii) tell me how you never prayed.

Tell me you were never answered in quite the right order.
      i) Longing finally realised.
      ii) This, as good a night as one could wish.

after years of nothing & this// the icarus of exits// the most intimate denial// there doesn't seem to be a compromise that does not end in a farewell// I will miss you// I will miss you// I will miss you most// I am done with this season & it is done with me// if I could disappear // for every year you have carried this with you// I would.//

Vanishing Point

Are you looking for
heaven?
I   hope
you find solace in answers.

Children without access to
water were taught to swim
in schoolyards laid bare
against the concrete Given
no first hand knowledge
of drowning, some things
you need to learn on your
own. Some locks do not
burden themselves with
open. Sometimes is an
analogue for almost.

In the days after the
damage, where were you? I
get the feeling you are
disappearing again.

Days sour. Like butter
spread thin & never to
the edges. There may be
more cohesive reasoning
but I believe, having never
taught   themselves
the delicate language
of fraught, your parents
wrote you speeding tickets
instead of birthday cards.

It's   no   surprise
you never learned slow,
Our   missing   person
posters' colours have
deliquesced into a cyan,
magenta & yellow autumn,
A hereditary lost & found.
Contact   details
accumulate, pool uselessly,
beneath telephone poles,
where they pointed you in
the direction of us.

Now the phone numbers
are discalculated, the top
heavy fractions of screened
calls have been simplified. I
heard you called
the answer to unbalanced
sums. Heard only the hiss
of   losses,   static,   &
grasshoppers.

Some   response   was
a tautology you learned to
live with. I don't think you
ever questioned the where
of *gone* when you found
out you lost something,
did you?

In those hospital months,
where the calendar didn't
fit my shoulders.

Those backless-gown couture
periods, you spent with paper
cup   hands   rubbing
confessions   from   lemon
eyes.

My eyes were bigger than
your stomach, that's true at
least. It's not important. The
one remove I wore in the
hope you would notice me at
any distance.

Caught in the grieving of
one another we are congruent.
Our abject tessellates.

It's good to see you again

I'm happy you're happy

I tell myself this so I can sleep at night.

Cupio dissolvi*

if there   is strength it lies
in   numbers. All   that counting
can   teach you about   drinking

away a year & being lost
for a   decade
is you abandon yourself
               to passion & give birth to your body as
                                       ruins
there is the strange reluctance of teeth epilogues & censorship blooms
       in your collapsing collarbone

eat birds that flew from your mouth whole
your   tongue   an epitaph
you copied the sentiment of from lovers who left before
you   had a   chance to   ascertain what distance meant
flocks of children & their amicable past swallowed whole by the telephone

                    voicemail eulogy†
does not   the body crave what it too destroys?
how catastrophic   & humble
the prophecy of our own   making is
the aspirational failings of history & haunted nuance.

two houses collapse   unable to take the weight
you're saving up to feel something   redemption in place of closure
if you make it   one more week   you can get enough
self loathing   for the both of us

---

*Coartr autem e duobus desiderium habens dissolvi et cum Christo esse multo magis melius / permanere autem in carne magis necessarium est propter vos.
Translation: I am straitened between two: having a desire to be dissolved & to be with Christ, a thing by far the better: But to abide still in the flesh, is needful for you.

Infomercial from the throat of a whale

"Take me up. & cast me forth into the sea; so shall the sea be calm unto you: for I know that for my sake this great tempest is upon you". - Jonah 1.12

In the stomach of a torrent you learn how to deify yourself whilst explaining to those caught at your funeral that this is just a misunderstanding. Is this how you plan your resurrection going?

Remember. A river births itself into a flood because it has nothing better to do, learns the limits of receding by looking into itself. Only on retreat into the empty does it become a river again.

If you believe in yourself, maybe you will never die. Body rotten from the aching womb of a drought & laid to rest for a decade protesting that you are alive.

Remember. The boy becomes a man in lieu of anything better to become. You spend a lot of time dead. You take up space with all the survival you ain't doing, till someone hauls you out of this compromise & you call it an awakening. Remember. The boy who became a mouth agape at the world choking on miracles. Remember, with a body made up from every dead version of you, you may not look like the messiah but you do bear a passing resemblance to the promised land.

If a man can't cross the same river twice, are you a different man or were they a different river? A wicked & adulterous generation asks for a sign & you, who have been born from the throat of a whale, look like as good a messenger as any.

Remember to tell those that bring you forth that they owe you an education for all the good it will do. Cry out in drowned tongues you demand an entire world of them. A world that you cannot give them. We have found you half digested in the stomach of a whale. We expect the most of you, bile covered miracle, rot born messiah. We expect you to know exactly what we need.

final resort

On the street dressed in GoFundMe's, petitions & forgiveness; genuine Turin rags
from the local goodwill store & with a cardboard box set up as a desk
Jesus tried to sell me a holiday. He wore a t shirt that read:
   solidarity forever with all oppressed people. Neither of us are convinced
the blood on his hands is just from picking at the scabs in his wrist,
his name has been used a lot for any number of things.

He proudly displays colorful postcards from the various countries where they
sacrifice people for being like rainbows, shows me his hat, made local, that says:
   oppression is the only reliable export of colonialism.

He says I have the look in my eye of *someone who wants different*, offers a road
strewn with palms, but we both know neither of us will ever take it.
Or perhaps instead, the Via Dolorosa for the adventurous type, the luggage limit
is an inconvenience, but everyone's got their cross to bear.

He says *There is a package deal on self-catering cease-fires though*
   they don't offer a refund in the event of cancellations. You have bomb shelters
   on your lips so might I recommend a country so far removed
   they speak the profiteering language of both sides-ing the vacation,
   whilst arming the hotel staff. Pretending both arrival & return are equally
   valuable. I can't recommend any good travel providers; they ask for neutrality.
   They call it a conflict but really, it's a tax haven. There's special offers
   on this day of tears.

   The owners summer in poverty & get very involved in vibrant local traditions
   by growing laurel groves in bombsites & burying their dead in oil reserves so
   they have a claim to it.
he says *They'll bail out the industry. I'm in no danger.* I can't distance myself from it
but it's *difficult to imagine more pristine beaches if you don't mind the occasional lost*
   tourist wandering up from the tides. They tread in my footprints you know?
   So it looks like they were never there. Looks like I carried them
   & abandoned them.

You can tell by this point his body is barely holding back the tears

> *I'm a native of the holy land, if you find where I died - visit the catacombs they made of the hospitals, send me a postcard. Tell me you wish you weren't there. The economy of second homes turned everywhere a no-fly zone I can barely turn a profit.*

He waves *Hello! I'm Icarus. Don't you recognise me?* at a passer-by & I'm not convinced he's mistaken. Take on the guise of someone selling sun to foreigners often enough & you too will have seas named after your grave.

You have to pity a man like that, everything done that he never agreed to. He tells me next time he'll *come back as a woman* & I believe him though I don't tell him how much more they'll hurt him because of it. He sings a lonely song of Magdalen & I buy an Easter weekend getaway, three grams of it, but I know I'll never take it. I have everything I need right here.

SINNER

Recant. Turn the body from a vessel into the airing of an unspoken grievance. Run. This isn't bravery – but failure masquerading as trying. There's no sense of occasion in lasts. Tell me, what is god to an addict? What is redemption to monsters? What is this demand but a position of piety instead of cruel & necessary knowledge?

In searching for answers, my hands become hard shoulders, pressed into the service of interrupting palms. This awkward allographacy †, the strange biology of a body denying itself & becoming something altogether different. Gutless, chitinous consequence. Wound parasite. Asphalt maelstrom of body in excess. I belong to smoke. To salt & shadow. To the monsters I became after long years of praying to myself.

As an addict you eschew glory for the sake of being unknown. Obscurity is a necessary sacrifice offered to the nights spent forgetting which state you were in. I am a violent excuse for a friend. I am harm manifest. I am part famine, part excess. Can you tell me apart from monsters? Absentee creation myth. Chest of open doors. Collapse apologist.

Locusts will eat each other because they are scared of being eaten by other locusts. I tear the insect limbs from the feast of my thorax to feed myself & delay the inevitable. I want to swallow the history of my body till I decohere. I want to harvest every afterlife I'm owed & distil redemption into something palatable. Five hundred & thirty-nine sins uttered into being. All those long years gathered in a body desperate for touch, a corpse waiting to become.

Is there a point at which your monstrous is forgiven? What Samaritan would stop for the god of the ditch? I am asking if you believe that, whatever excavation has taken place, you trust me to have examined my past & made an informed verdict. Or would you prefer me to repent each time I am made anew in someone else's eyes? Glory to the pavement gods. This is how people like me don't pray for the end but reenact it.

Body as temple registered to offshore tax havens wondering why the inner child is starving

The god of my body is dead, tongue haunted by famine. I am crowdfunding his return. If you have ever devoted your ruin to a room empty of you, you will know how well this works. My body is a temple to the echoes left in the churches you abandoned. The crowded mouth of gospel holds no space for problems like me.

My body was a temple but I was never the god it was devoted to, rather to the rhetoric of accidents, to the interior design of pornography, the inherent disgust the mirror holds, & the removal of our wisest teeth. Why hold a graveyard responsible for a body that never learned the ritual of burial? My body was a temple to the colour pink & raw flesh, to another fortune spent on wishing wells, to sleep sermons & clairvoyance.

Sacrosanct, I renovate myself; temple to 3am & hope, I know how to lie. I know when to become Holy mason of undesign. Prosaic. Dreaming dirty was a chore. I call myself: temple to Paris as an afterthought. Make my body temple to gaslighting yourself & forgetting. Promise my body the long lonely of worship. I revere the planning permission of touching myself because no one else will.

If the god of your body is dead, is the church & all it's work made worthless?

My body, ruined by saviours. My body begging to be taught how to be immortal since you're so good at it, my body surgery derelict, historic removal, here's everyone who believed in you once. Why do we perpetuate at the cost of others? Hey gimme that temple, I'm talking to you.

god fragment II: Passage of Rites

Until the hallway features in a narrative
you have not talked fully on the transition of leaving.
Until the hallway, Witness to Exits,
Patron of Returning, Paradox of Journeys,
is exalted the way it deserves,

the way it was one time became
the last thing someone saw,
the premature of closed doors.
Until the hallway is acknowledged
as the poor, if only, excuse for a shrine to motion
there will be no resolve. The rain.
The rain intervenes, checks visas,

have you been given leave to go?
Have you considered how the house
will process your departure?
I believe it will worship
the altar of your absence

placed firmly in the shoe rack.

NEW TESTAMENT

I'm not looking for god, I found them. Now it's my turn to hide

What if you & the saviour of mankind mutually agree you should see other people? You want different things & eking this out further is just a clever way to deny that neither of you are fit for purpose?

What if you agree to give up on god? Quit god? Cold turkey & absence god. The god of one remove & it's not you it's me god. The Oh god of Denial, the lament of a Gone god. The Doubting Thomas Prayer for a Hide & Seek god. Lost god. The I Can't Commit Right Now, I Have A Lot of Stuff Going on Emotionally god, the At A Different Time This Might Have Worked god. God who left you, after the late shift, ten fathoms tall in heels, god who called you all the names under the sun & god who held his hand to the griddle because can't you see he loves you. What if you say, no more god? What if you deny him outright, put your foot down & turn away to seek something, anything else.

But then he appears on the first day you do? A bottle full of hymns & a crazy idea that sounds like he stole it verbatim from a heist movie you're pretty sure he put on that time he came over for Netflix & chill & there was no chill & promises he could do better. What if you sleep with god cradled in your chest one last time then in the morning you tell him you won't let him use you this way again? Tell him cleanliness must be as far away from godliness as can be.

What happens if mere moments after saying it, a prayer-inducing tragedy comes along & he leaves & you find yourself? What if your friends are churches? What if this is the last you see of him? What if years later, after you have flirted with pantheons; held others' psalms close to your mouth & whispered the holy body of some other Ghost into shoulders in motel rooms; after awkward moments avoiding miracles opposite you, pretending you didn't see them because you had elsewhere to be. Later, after occasional nights spent on the hood of your car, communion wine drunk & staring at the skies looking for someone, as between your legs another someone murmurs a sermon. Later, after sedentary texts, the administrative process of border disputes,

avoiding direct contact, splitting friends evenly, heart reacts to big life moments &
birthday phone calls two days after the fact his holy brother calls you & says
*I know you used to be close & I'm sorry it took me so long to tell you. But god
passed away in their sleep on Tuesday morning & the funeral is next week. They would
have wanted you to be there so be there.*

What if the numbness is more surprising than the grief? What if you arrive at god's
funeral, forget the words to the eulogy & instead stare at space, think of nothing
you can do other than note you expected this place of worship to be more full?
That you had heard everyone would be there & there are spaces between the few
mourners on the pews? What if the only recognisable objects are single pairs
of footprints & parted seas to the exit? It can be lonely, to even be in the presence
of this defined a lack of mourning. How even the angels have ceased their singing
& are just humming & pretending to know the words, same as the rest of us.

What do you do if, whilst sitting thinking following the service, your cup filled
with seawater, because you don't drink no more, a prophet approaches
from the revelling protest of fresh atheists, floating amicably having altogether decided
they will now deny gravity, & says here, he wanted you to have this? & hands you
a throne, a bloodline, three verdigrised coins, a crown, a lamb, a sceptre or whatever
symbol you think is the best metaphor for power, before disappearing back into
the cowering pack of mourners. Leaving you with your hollow thoughts.

Will you pretend to grieve, when you know that absence is no different from presence
when there is never an answer? When your name is the only god you ever need.
Are you really going to tell me you are still mourning your holy, or will you show me
your miracles?

god fragment III: how to find the body

bear witness to the contingencies of worship.
did you grow into your neck?
your accent - a negotiation of prayer & doubt.
the pavement comments on your family resemblance
to leaving - if you remain, expect nothing
more than to stage an intervention on returning.
this wretched body of ours is a liminal space
between nearly & enough.

I believe in you & your coping mechanisms

speak my railway spine i beg you,
staircase anachronistic representation
of how we used to find ourselves always reaching.
i am searching for the secrets of your failsafes in your second hand life
unsettled. unsung. there are teeth in your throat.
begging to be ground. comfort is a martyr. i am rooted
an evolution in discourse. i don't want to
excuse myself for the sake of gaps

the etiquette of grieving requires making yourself finite

a prophet approaches wearing the world
like a grievance. wearing the collar
of conflict from trying too much
i want you to know what i forgive you for
bear witness to your altar of soft. skin blooms &
i have found the body of god.
the whale fall of a deity & we are
hungry, gorging on the remnants

calling ourselves holy.

My Name Is Dispute

I don't tell you how often I think of setting myself on fire. Once a week me & the other arsonists who thought ourselves firefighters sit in circles & hold the warmth of coffee against our weakness. We do not talk of kindling. We do not talk of the cold, or our real names, instead we hold our coffee cups like promises. We listen to one another. We talk. & at first I tell them:

> *I know exactly how it feels when the bottle calls you a god.*

It is only when I listen I learn my name means
> *two gods having a conversation.*

One man said his name meant he was *the boy who ate what was given to him.*
He learnt to starve himself by eating himself & how to become an argument.

My name means choke.

My name means dispute.

My name means because.

These definitions are proof of how people like us are prone to decay; how failure is a common result of escapism; how, for all my bravado, I am no end; I'm just a beginning that doesn't know the start is over yet.

When the only thing you stand to inherit from your name is violent history you will understand the need to find sobriquets. How you must always call the last move before you make them & how I name myself burden.

I am surrender swallowed in the absence of sustenance (repeat)
I am surrender swallowing the absence of sustenance (repeat)
I am surrender swallowed in the absence of sustenance (repeat)
                                        repeat until no longer necessary.

We do not talk of how we know each other better than our real names. We do not talk of how if this don't kill me then nothing will, because my name means I am immortal. Because I will live forever in the hope of becoming a memory. Because there will never be a time I don't pray for the end. If I could be nearly half the man I thought I was, it would have to suffice.

But my name is *paradoxes caused by the differences between who I was & who I am.* My name is *everything I loved went the wrong way because it followed me* & I never revealed the trick of not stepping on the cracks in paving slabs or to remember to wake up before you hit the ground. The most frequently heard name called out on the way down is

  so far so good.

I can tell you from experience anyone's name can mean falling.

So tell people who have lost themselves to get better at finding & you will understand why tomorrow is a promise we can't make so today will have to suffice.
I am no end.
I am *no* end.

I'm just a beginning that doesn't know what the next step is yet, I'm a prologue to better days that don't end just because I do. I am Saint of absent dialogues & god of unhealed wounds. Four years is a long time to remain nameless. But it is better than a decade spent without deserving one.
So my name is

  this doesn't feel like a resolution   *because it isn't one.*

From the Book of Just you Fucking Wait

1. Places where your body is not, look like halfway houses for sermons. 2. Wanting to leave does not mean you are gone. 3. We are compromises of the encore. 4. Our skin graffitied. 5. Our scars shibboleths. 6. Are trespassers here in god's country & this exile reads like it was written as a satire. 7. Arguably, this is enlightenment by proxy. 8. Arguably, this short sleeve language speaks in the uncomfortable tongue of the living.

—

9. If we were immortal then death would be welcome. 10. No one is a prescription for the way you wear your wounds. 11. I'm a testament. 12. You can be a map without leaving. 13. I am a testament. 14. Bodies are god's least answerable questions. 15. I'm a testament. 16. You can sign off your letters 17. *warm regards, the higher power you never had.* 17. & still stay. 19. Today autocorrects your name to *missing* 20. & you have to check to see if you are dead.

—

21. & Lo. 22. The day rises on a moment you no longer want to erase. 23. You find the means to no end you were searching for. 24. You, the recipient of phantom limbs 25. Do you hate with donated fists? 26. Is your violence inherited? 27. Is your name a boundary you will not cross? 28. O'er the land a voice echoes. 29. You will make it. 30. You must.

A man lies in an empty field. an unopened bag beside him

The crop most resistant to drought is desire. The empty silos & the starving are searching for answers. You cultivated void with purpose, pews of safety mechanisms, empty of people. The choir sings for the wet season, hopes for the flood.

You are forest fires set to prevent forest fires the immaculate conception of by any means necessary. You never let yourself grow fallow.

Communion is a hard time to be in recovery, confessional is a small box to learn bloodlust.

In temples built to your fear of balance, those hungry for sacrament gather, the censer bearer's smoke reaching the three ring release system of parachutes.

Here, the congregation that looked like a safety net will start to make sense. You always were so good made disaster seem like it deserved an encore. You always were so good at martyrdom for the sake of applause. You always were so good at falling.

On the one hand you hope that there is a single set of footprints because you were carried, in the other, you hold a ripcord.

Cup your palms, to receive blessings & miss the point. This felt like a second chance.
But redemption is often the unpacking of something to ensure that it will fit back in, redemption is often emptying yourself of everything to make enough room to acknowledge

the replacing of everything unpacked. If you are

nothing, do not be surprised if you have removed an emptiness to replace it with an audience that will not be satisfied till you are exsanguinate.

god fragment IV: Piano Tuner of Earthquakes

This archive footage is courtesy of my vacant mouth. If the recipient's pulse is missing you must lend him yours. This corridor has been twinned with the tendons in my neck & the promise that we will map ourselves in fire exits. Emergency protocols for tenderness willing, I will escape this loss.

This picture shows me giving me no time to explain myself. Nursing a North Carolina shaped hole in my Dakota heart where my reflection used to be. The mirror ceases its staring competition. I get the feeling you are disappearing. You did yourself a disservice in apologising. There is nothing to answer for in the reciprocation of leaving. You have spent too long in being a souvenir but the piano ♒ is asking questions of the hallway. Again.

The god of heights is no match for the reality of landings but afraid is where we have been for far too long. Replacing the floorboards in your home is just a metaphor for your fear of losing. There is no honour in being an accident. This is what to do in case you find out you are dead.

Weakerthan

Realising the way the conversation was headed, instead of speaking, I cited my pockets as an escape plan to steady myself & found remnants of the car crashes we left of one another in 2006 & again in 2012. Found how we called that damage because & never did much about it. I found that touch is my hands' way of saying I can't. I found someone else's knuckles cracked in the percussion of impatient punchlines, found the osteoporosis of faltering conversation & the great impression you do of a good friend but promptly lost it again.

I carried the argument we had outside the house of an acquaintance with me ever since, & it's no surprise to find it there still. I have seen you with your hands buried so often I thought you too would have something to show but all you let me see is some sleight of hand. Blaming it on bottled fathers & the compromise of distance you said scarecrows had reasons enough to return to their blackbird wives, said deserts wore petrichor as cologne to seduce lost travelers & that you had no time to be found.

You said that my searching for responses was the collateral damage of too many questions & you were sick of my friendly fire need for answers. The reason you never got back to me with closure was due to the white noise of cognitive dissonance you said.

My pockets empty further devoid themselves of errant postcards & lying in bathtubs that time in 2005 remove the memories of the brickwork of jazz & swing, your inchoate step, the brazen wake up calls hung by an honourable man seeing no need for change exiling a narrative I tried to force. Evict my inability to see the failures were mine. Pockets will turn themselves out, acknowledge a truth I find hard to stomach or give name to. Will leave only a truth I find hard to covet. Will leave only my hands empty of yours & of leaving.

How to turn an injury claim into a cult

Did you know that injury has a profit margin? If your father is found in deadman's curves then wounds are a garish aesthetic we disguise our almost with. As you wait for the other driver to make it safely from the wreckage of his vehicle, dip fingers in the broken glass of wing mirrors & drivers' side windows. Adorn your injuries with diamonds. Ornamental agony. Embellished finery in your wrists. Ensure you are alive, bedecked in the ritual beauty of survival. This looks like lying because it almost is.

Did you know that worship is where we are asked to bear witness to our warm wet insides? Your body undoes seatbelts & flings open doors any time self reflection gets too close to the bone, allowing you to escape the burning wreck you could be & instead offers you the escape of being an organ donor. Acknowledge the questions of inheritance. How fast were you lying the last time you asked this? Is this your crisis? Would you recognise your past lives? Would you want to? Did you know that the reason people experience whiplash is due to the body bracing itself against the impact? It has nothing to do with external pressures but it is, ultimately, your body saving itself from itself.

Did you know that if you crawl from the wreckage of a burning vehicle, you can still turn it into a story about salvation? You can explain you were on the way to drive-thru chapel mothers who teach that men only love to prove themselves worthy of being redeemed. But no one is obliged to believe you. People treat you with some kind of reverence when you donate your organs pre mortem. They do this so they might touch the scars of your generosity.

Watch them look up lovingly, from their knees. Lips pressed to your hips & slide their fingers inside the open of you. It will feel like the spear of Longinus. It will feel like the touch of a lover. Both of these things are true - for a given value of true. Know that not only are wounds & affection interchangeable but also that people call this cruelty kindness & expect thanks.

You will find yourself walking, three people wrist deep in your rib cage, sizing you up though never, ever asking outright for the organs they yearn for. The kidney, the lungs & the holy guts. This autopsy is a baptism. This moment of clarity is donated for scientific purposes. Staging the greatest comeback since Lazarus. body stitched up & still holy, to make people believe in you. To ensure no one can doubt your recidivism is an agony. An agony you are done with.

This is how to profit off your own ugly rebirth. Your lover is a mechanic who sucks his teeth every time you kiss him & tells you it will be expensive & it always is. This is the way to convert the write offs of your body. Leaving friendship shaped holes in traffic, leaving backseat drivers who swallow their teeth to forswear the hindsight radio preaches, leaving the hard work of believing to everyone else. Become a roadside attraction to grieving pilgrims, sell souvenirs, stained-bandages-turned-turin-shrouds as tea towels, your own face missing from them, splinters of bone masquerading as fragments of the cross & locus reports of last moments that tell a version of the truth. The burden of knowing that it isn't an ignoble thing to ask to die.

Not if you don't really mean it.

Netflix & chill, only make it existential

If anyone wants to span the gaps
between my ribs. The bone & breath where capture is
absent. To find
failure's contortionism, to count

each protrusion like it's their own,
you are welcome. It will mean I don't have to
trap fingers in the bars
of cages I keep myself safe in. I have had enough
           of searching for proof that I am living. In my skin
excuses have no room to be.

Doubt's line of questioning seldom makes
for satisfying responses.
My body,
           in this way, is evidence
           of caution,
my body,
           in this way, is,
           if not a crime scene,
                      then at least a suspect.

Superlatives heal slowest.

In the spaces between punches
  either exchanged   or delivered, there is only a void.

In this way we are all guilty
of looking for responses, or answers,
or redemption, in the lives of others. Ignorance
adores a vacuum.

Some wounds have no border patrols
& the divorce   of skin
from muscle   has left an open ended request
to corroborate   your version of events.

This is not intended
as an indictment for searching
          but the meat of answers
does not sustain the violence of looking.

Prove me innocent,
          the cold case,   of my body
                    & guilty verdicts fall apart.
                              Uncover, some tentative archaeology
                                        of what I was
                                                  prove that my life,

delicate still lingers

Priorities of Cannibalism

1. Prayer is a tupperware party where fleshy housewives caked in sorrow flagellate each other & swear their husbands will get better. Occasionally they allow the most photogenic orphans to become wet floor signs. The mourning of orgies lost to commerce is the most plaintive song you will hear. Whales write lengthy odes to it in abyss speech & baleen tongue. Apparently the prophets inside of the mouths of the whales who recite the poetry are well fed but their predictions are lacking. There are queues to fill the shoes of those lost in whale months.

2. There are these no smoking sections in heaven, which makes sense when you think of all the horny widows fucking the clergy but sometimes I just want a break from the neon halo above my head & my crypt keeper body. Sometimes I want to piano wire my testicles. Sometimes I think *if* I garotte myself they will make some pretty impressive art to commemorate the act.

3. Officially speaking three statues in the history of reliquaries have cried blood. Now they must weep on command; milk, sweat, bile, other bodily fluids. Whatever has harmed them. Whatever fulgent facade has been reaped of stone harvests. There's an etiquette in naming the removal of doubt. The priests are not allowed near the statues. They are the only thing the church holds sacred.

4. There are four subdivisions in the hierarchy of the church, three are dedicated to cloning god or at least harvesting the organs of whatever body they can make, the other is public relations & one tiny Franciscan monk bound to silence who works part time in HR. Absence requests are always denied which is odd considering. But we don't think too much of it - the reward comes after. This is written on the skin they took from apostates hundreds of years ago & made into tiny origami orchids therefore it is uncouth to question it.

5. The church has declined all requests for comment, says I can't prove nothing & sells fat babies in the gift shop as they usher you to the door. They label them half price miracles & perhaps they are.

Hellbent

Not in the name strengthened by the intercession of the Immaculate Concrete moment / Not in the name of the Mother of paving slabs / not of Blessed Monuments the Archangel / not you in the wake up call / not in the name of the Blessed Apostles denied us / & all the Saints / Not *your* mercy, lord, descending upon us / We need not in yours / The hope of us is not in vain / As great our hope in ourselves is defined / may we never need you / & may we not be snatched away & driven from the church of rock & hard places & / may we yet be redeemed by the steps we took too long in taking / & may he, with whom, in our great insolence, we still claim to be equal / realise we will not turn to you / may we seek no higher power than ourselves / Not the god of pick your own gospel, choose your own hate / not the god of trickle down economics posing as justification for poverty / not the god of plausible deniability / not the god of relapse / not the god of premium access redemption / nor the god of the body of an eight year old child / not the god of government / not the decaying god bastard of billionaires / not the god of state sanctioned apocalypses / nor the god of emergencies / & certainly not the god of apathy / nor god of the last minute change of hearts for murderers & priests / nor the god who has power to give life after death & rest after work & yet does not / because there is no other god than thee / so we turn our back on you / god / & though we know there can be no other / know it's not the morning that compels us nor more the night / to believe in anything but you / not thee who says he wants all men to be saved / or to come to the knowledge of the truth / when instead we can offer just one more cup of flesh / strip the prayer from our bones / find our own glut / We are told the god of abandoned demands this of us / though his work is barren / & the god of blades & the son of knives commands us / though his work is absent / & the holy ghost of any god who will listen / commands us still / & we ask / what did this book ever do for us but set impossible standards / & show us how to disappoint them / & show us dead words made flesh / & command our envy, becoming / obedient even unto death / The sacred Neon of the Cross commands us / as does the man standing outside with the vestments commanding we are not to enter / this is not indicative of the body god, nor of the concessions / nor of the angels / nor of those well meaning questions / that tie us into knots / nor ever, ever of the intervention of those who would undo us rather than see us free / The glorious Mother Virgin commands us / & she who by her humility & from the cunt moment of her

Immaculate Inconvenience crushed thy proud head / The faith of the holy apostles - Liver Failure & Rent Due / & of the other Apostles commands us / The blood of martyrs & the pious intercession of all our errant Saints command us / Thus, cursed dragon, & you, diabolical legion / we accept ourselves by the livid god / & by the defragment god / & by the lotus seed god / & by the god who so needed to be loved by those he broke / he killed his only son / Munchausen by proxy for an arbitrary god / told every soul grieving on his behalf that by believing in him they might not perish but have life everlasting / stop deceiving yourself & pouring out to them the poison of eternal damnation / god / is this how you pictured thy intervention going / Watch us stoop beneath the all-powerful hand of god / watch us tremble & flee when we invoke the holy & terrible name of *ourselves* / this name which trembles / this name to which the submissive / the wet & the unwieldy of heaven are humbly grateful / this name which the addicts & the merchants praise unceasingly repeating / Holy, Holy, Deign, O Lord, to deny us thy powerful protection / do we beseech thee through Jesus Christ our Lord / to deliver us, O Lord? / Envelop thy razor wire home inside us lord / if our speech slurs & our words tremble / does that negate our prayer? / not my god, lord / not my god / no longer of rhetoric / but of knives & know how / No longer of the line of Saints but of the yearning / not to live any more lies / We beseech thee to ignore us / all we'll ever ask of you / deny us visions of what might be & you / must not turn away but acknowledge / it is not real / this feeling of not being you / lord have mercy on those who cannot accept the things we cannot change / who cannot change / whose circumstance is more powerful than us / & lord who put us in that position help yourself to the glut of our ancestors / gorge yourself fat on our history / since that's what you need of us / & try to deliver us / lord of oaths & flies the broken & condemned things / lord of filicide / of jump scares, twist endings & cruel deceitful lies / & we're afraid in ways that only the dispossessed can really know / so ask if you'll take the madness inside us & argue / the world is a horrendous catalogue of errors that started off badly & went worse / & we can still taste the joy of it lingering on our asphalt tongues/ & there is still joy but little / so precious little in these days of carcrashes & traffic fathers / so we tell ourselves / swallow the road, boy / history is a bridge we must cross / our spines will curve up to meet our losses / & we must know how to differentiate / Our brawler bodies built for fighting / love the emergency of our existing / We need not of you / god / only of us.

To Praise Prosthesis: Destruction as the cause of coming into being[1]

I am a many faced god
breech born into the void of my body.
Weary of my own need for worship,
tired of my own absence, of retribution.
From here, I see no power higher than me.

If you, like me, remember the time you could not exist
you are forgiven for seceding from the empire of the barely living.
For granting sanctuary to questions who can fuck away the pain by becoming it.
For renovating the empty space in open arms,
a haven for self saboteurs, solace from the flood.

If you remember being imprisoned, your hands deliquescing,
the fault of burning water & asking answers of empties,
you are forgiven.
The second favourite son lost himself in the desert
but his friends never appeared to him as oases, like yours did.

Denial is the slow revelation of god's will.
There's no emanation of judgement
from torn ligaments in hands
grown tired of catching ourselves.

Change our clothes to show willing
sacrifice skin & wear thorns.
Deny the pantomime of our bodies
the performative cruelty of our existing.
Once more sing our own survival song
Just one more day
                    just one more day can't hurt.

god fragment V: Of waiting rooms

Close. Close. Closer this museum sickness, familiar disease.
I am loathe to admit there's no language made for this
but in accepting how heavy the gone of you is
I have moved on, haven't I? haven't I? haven't I?
haven of espresso hands & flame, clutching guilt complexes & understanding
wrapped a body in arms that knew not how to accept
the spaces you occupied are now filled with knives.

Far, far, farther away I can acknowledge
by demanding myself to be present
by being a thing of doors
& exits & wolves & warning signs I have made a difference.
Content to have honoured

promises to brick walls, the dead & the living
I can rust. I can rest. I can make amends.
A Lament:

If I forgot the sound of your voice,
& find that leaving is the body's way
of proving that it lived,

can I forget about you
& move on?

THE PHARASEES, THE PROPHETS, THE UNBURDEN, THE RECANTATION

portrait of our lady of sorrows on fire

prayers* are the lips of heaven parted from us having left it. say love me & i will forget about god; the arborvitae forever blooming in the cusp of our chests; the awkward of our inviting & the refusals of calendars to accept the gone of you. Almost seven years to the day since I found you never refused to be translated by the violence of eulogies but left us instead to recite all the names we give to your deep rest, I still long for the quiet of our knowing. Friendship as evergreen, as iodine sunset; Season of missing, year of gone. I owe you.

*for prayer say instead:
1. spring blossoms dismantled by an eventual winter.
2. peace processes rendered obsolete by time.
3. lighthouses coveted by the sorrow of the sea;
   dismantled by need; on fire from no maintenance.
4. necessary.

Saint of morrow & of missing

what is gained by refusing your place
in the scheme of things
are you so ready to believe
all the horror told in your wake
god of paper cuts & brambles
a circle of dead ants is not a cult
the long exposure worship
of an empty space where a friend was
the key to this is yet
the key to this is not letting yourself

Saviour of Midwest dive bars

(after Leon Priestnall's poem "Johnny")

Baby tell me the taste of your BMI,
I want to finance your insecurities.
to find a way in to make you believe in me,
to play your vulnerable off your scepticism.

Tell me your credit card details & how you can't quit
buying running shoes or cinnamon rolls or artisan candles
or self help books or furniture upcycled from less impressive furniture.

Do you read poetry? Do you detest anything?
Do you cast stones? Do you ever wonder if people's taste
in sci-fi movies tells you about how well they'd weather an apocalypse?
Would you prefer if their taste means they fuck good,

or do you focus more on if it would make them a better father?
Do you feel worthy?
Do you confess your sins?
Or do you save it for the intimacy of infinite nights
spent talking to outlines that you hope are awake?
When you are on your knees is it worship or penitence you're feeling?
Do you make graven images of the bodies of ex lovers?
Do you lock your life when you leave it?
Do you double check doors?
Do you remember where you last had it?

Baby do you drink? Are you rye or persimmons?

Does the chiaroscuro of your ribs against the bar mean you are open

to believe in something better? Something for the group chat to tell

your friends.

My blood turned to wine a long time ago.

I've already asked that you consummate this cannibalism

by taking my words as gospel.

It might not have sounded like that when I said it

but baby, I promise that is what I was asking.

I promise I sext in scripture.

I promise I touch myself in Revelations

Have you ever felt worthy?

Baby, do you know the I Am?

Has your tongue pulled *my* name out

of the woodwork yet?

Kiss me & I'll fix you a drink.

Are you the kind of person who goes home

with someone they don't know

on the first night you meet?

Daddy's little burning bush,

If I were to let you suck my tongue, would you be grateful?

Daddy's favourite lost apostle

if you weren't looking for saving what brought you here?

Baby, have you ever felt you were worthy?

My name is Jesus but you can call me *in the morning*.

The boy with no hands

Did you ever learn to blow smoke rings?
I taught myself how to dissipate in summer evenings,
how to induce a phobia & count cobwebs between knuckle joints.

  I got it wrong this time round.
  I have found the last scraps of a diary,
  it is written in someone else's hand
  but I'm certain it's yours.
  The dreams are oversized.

I heard once of someone who wanted to be a saint so badly
he lost everything to ensure he could be the patron of finding
& spent the rest of his life trying to undo his own desires.

  What were you praying about?
  That time you twisted
  cornrows into halos & chewed grass,
  blew seeds from the corner of your mouth,
  said you would be something someday. *Was it this?*
  I've spent a lot of time praying over something too.

Did I ever thank you for picking me up,
a boy indiscernible
from the sofa he was sitting on?
I get the feeling
you are disappearing again.

I believe I know how to love better than most
& that is why I don't.
If there is redemption in the touch of others,
I can't. I'm frightened of forgetting.

Do you think it's possible to hate yourself
for something you don't know if you did?
I think it is & I do.

You were a fine lesson to be taught,
days spent at phone calls' end,
unsure which side was convincing the other to stay
a little while longer.

It has been so many days since my last confession
& *someday* still sounds like an analogue for almost.
I'm frightened that nostalgia is my apology
for never telling those I love
that I am giving up.

From the Book of Job

The Patron Saint of Second Chances Jumps Back into the Fire

Shadrach said to Abendego
  I don't feel these burns brother, do you?
as Mishael hid his palms.

I'm not struggling to breathe.
I'm rewilding my lungs.
This isn't praying.
its reclaiming.
This isn't searching for.
This is hiding from.

The patron saint of second chances
is an addict to the narrative of burning
before he is an addict to anything else.

The other figure with us in the flames
is often just a coincidence. There's no need to be concerned
The redemptive process is not a necessity
not if you don't mean it

more convincing scripture exists elsewhere
written in breath on mirrors I'm disappearing in.
  but I try setting myself on fire again
   Because today, *I will not*
is the *remains to be seen* of grieving.

when one has lived with prophecy so long, the prediction becomes more comfort than the realisation

58

god Kintsugi I: fifty shades of grace

We are reconnecting awkwardly at the body festival. The celebration of bones. & find, as usual, we are the only ones who have bought our gods with us & somehow still know the need of holy. Of all the things you can ask of someone, sometimes absence is the most needed. I was happy to give it but today is one of those days where I feel it right to check if my missing is what you need in this moment. There's a want in us both for nostalgia & since we are comparing the wounds left by the leaving of gods it still bears saying; if I destroy god's house because I didn't know how not to - it doesn't make god's house less destroyed. I'll not minimize the trauma wrought by the relics of holy leaving. Despite the circumstances it feels disingenuous & painful to navigate all the damage of my name so I'll leave it to you to speak beginnings. Small comfort, the throat of lost words. We find a shorthand into the phatic. The unknowing of our grieving. Ways to broach the absence of a shared past. But both still sit on our hands for fear of what we might do with them & eat with difficulty. Both still make bridges of bone for better days. Both still searching for fragments of openings & only finding closure. We swap our sinner's mouths for cello strings, draw cigarettes legato to punctuate our slow narrative & I wonder if this is just how we always talked. 15 years on & I am only now learning the underhanded etiquette of our lung song. Concrete obdurate loss. We'll argue tender this is just a one off & not make too much of losing faith. I am quiet in my demand. Content of circumstance & settled of uncommon times. None more heavy feels the burden of redemption than an addict & this is more brief amnesty than true absolution. But I'll take it. I'll never be able to atone for never my getting help when I needed to, but here, laying our friend to rest I can acknowledge the brief sanctuary made of conversation & the respite of pronouns like our So, so long to the things I thought would save me. I'll leave this intermission a quiet remand - just ask if there must be amends, let them be gentle. If we are to reach agreements on custody, let them be honest. If you never talk to me again, it will have been enough.

Saint of Knives & other apocrypha from forgotten apostles

I'm celebrating as if the ground isn't full.

You can't say the earth is healing // and not notice the wounds // stones blooming from these scars // are inscribed with declarations of love // no don't tell me you are glad I made it // don't say today is enough // when tomorrow I plant rituals//where a friend should have grown.

A hush where there was a person becomes an echo becomes an enjambment. In the between of prophecies live people who should be.

Possibility nexuses, nothing specific predicted about them, just that they will.

Stage blades can still do damage & the monologue that autumn deserves is delivered best by breathing underwater, a drowned dirge to wet winters. Rise, rise, rise! Hail! The Saint of Knives! Their first gospel read simply:

Terms of endearment can be shibboleths, held in the mouth of those who want not to love, a mouth, a throat, a thinly veiled swallow that has sought to regurgitate holiness, a tongue as an absence in another's mouth, a tongue in someone else's mouth as a replacement for something prophetic.

As it is written so it isn't, as it is written why shouldn't it be denied?

rot blooms in the vestibule

Some lies work best on paper, but then open secrets are cursed secrets.

The smartest trick ever pulled was convincing us we didn't exist. All hail! The Saint of Knives! Protesting the disarmament of dissenting voices. Folding petitions from the dead to prevent overcrowding. Injuries are horizons & battlefields are corporate logos. People don't become statistics, we make them.

life is the most common cause of death but not the only extant one. grief needs a saviour if only to reconcile it with our habit of interring today in lies that we tell ourselves of tomorrow

The violins inherit the system, dismantle it & play a tune to packed out dance floors that let us forget ourselves. In forgetting ourselves we are reminded of the first book of the Saint of Knives.

Every dance move is explicit. Every tender touch or erstwhile fuck a prayer in some way.

When we kiss we are saying:

I am an analogy for you. Outside of safety, outside here, holy alone & still searching. Teach me we're worth it. Into the summer where the streets, measured in tennis shoes & doc martens, are stuck to the sky like a tongue toothing the wound where a bite used to be.

Iammendment:

This isn't supposed to be inspiring, medical texts seldom are, so why should the vagaries of lust, written in the shorthand of someone who may orr may not have existed, encourage us to do anything other than than observe that to interact is human and necessary?

Love can be a protest, but sometimes living as a marginalisation is sufficient.

The second book of the Saint of Knives never said anything. It is a blank page. Here in my own crabbed hand I write:

who needs to call a rose by any other name when I have a thorn in my side like you

This is as good a call to arms as any. Deny. Retract. Cross out & repent.

I never had you, I never had the comfort of you, I was never you.

Would similarly be an appropriate second verse. We can sing this loud as our bodies allow, but why allow such beauty to be placed in function when the form of knowing is so arbitrary?

say you meant it all along Say this is what you intended.

I predict we will forget & be glad of it, I predict that when this is translated, years from now, they will say that this *was* what was said, not what might have been. If the message is lost because someone misconstrues it's intention it doesn't have to be.

if we must grieve let us do so in our own way If we are forced not to. If we must manifest our loss as a significant other, let it be one with a kind face. Say you meant this all along.

Hail! The Saint of Knives! I predict you will be & that is enough.

This is all second hand knowledge, I have never even seen a crow

REDEEMER

Everything known about dying is from unreliable accounts. I am not recommending first hand experience but I am researching methods of resurrection. Rediscovering artifacts from the undertow teaches me better about swallowing evenings to build up a tolerance for the dark. In the morning I am renovating my body with stigmata so I become immune to knives. My skin smiles the keloid grin of a glutton of attrition.

The problem with not knowing the arcane of yourself is getting confused with who you could be. I've been fulfilling prophecies because I'm too scared to take chances. I can feel the succulent under my chest avoiding my gaze, & answer honestly that I have only ever been approximately human.

I dream of god killing himself. Turn my hands into blades for just such a purpose. They have to be god killing knives. I absolve my stomach in the shower & scrub my gentle soft clean of any guilt. My mouth is an empty nest, hollow of prophecy, where something good once was. If I am to offer my hands for anything, they must be hewn from my body. The callous, vicious rhetoric of self sacrifice in context of having nothing. I dare not ask either for crosses or consolations: I present myself before god, knowing I must kill him or become him, I open my heart to the grisly task. Behold my needs which I know not myself; see & do according to tender mercy ᛞ

If I have been made in his image then my hands are god weapons by design. If he has the means of killing himself then so do I. If I have been made with the intention to kill god, I must trust gods' holy script & not falter. Plunge my hands into the neck of god & lovingly, lovingly cradle his head as he disappears. I accept the mantle of god, though it's burdens are infinite. After everything it will be peaceful to have the power to make amends & no desire to do so. I adore all his purposes without knowing them; I am silent; I offer myself in sacrifice; I yield myself; I have no other desire than to accomplish what I am intended for. Teach me to pray. Pray there is a god in me. ←⊕

Does my awkward not marr the process of apotheosis? A man still held mortal by all the ways in which he went wrong. I was not cut out for this. I'm so almost sorry for the ghost I made him be & honour him as someone who cured me of sleep. It's nostalgic, to me, being used to seeing empty houses as part of my fathers work, disenfranchised bodies as real estate for the old ones.

I'm told I have it in me to change. In response I offer the solace that I am immune to knives. I am admired for how brave I am to accept my failings in such an artful way. Applause ripples the god body consuming itself in the eagerness of anonymity. I am told the mouths erupting in my skin are blessings that I didn't allow myself to feel the weight of. We limit ourselves to hungers we can manage. I'm told that if my body is mouths & knives then it is because I am chosen. I dare not ask what for. Not now. Not after all the prayers I have hit reply all to with *sure if you think it will change anything* . I'm told I can be a martyr. I respond - provided it means I make it out of this one alive

The Unique Grief of the Apostle of Bones

I don't even know where
you are buried.
The best kept secret
of your loss. I have no idea
if the greenstick fractures
that shaped my youth still
speak of you. I can't tell if
the mouth with the softest
voice, the one nestled
cenobitic in my chest,
the one that says
the cruellest things in the
sharpest of months still
garners your name with
the praise it deserves.
I wonder if,
when the crows attend
the service, they are aware
they heralded disaster,
the ivory images in temples
wept for grief, I wonder if
they still gather

to commemorate you,
least forgotten friend.
I never broke a bone
whether I meant to or not
The mouths in my torso
are quitetened by scarring,
the piece missing
has been declared obsolete
& made do without as if
never needed.
There *might be*
many rooms in my father's
houses. *There is a need for
crowsong*, demands
the horizon.
I can't stop reliving
your memory, but
I don't want to do this
alone anymore or again so
fled the nest & left mouths
empty. I suspect

everyone else does.
the hard work of
remembering
the broken boned
recuperating from silence
is not the same & I'm
hoarse under different
skies. Ones in which
you are not dead & I dont
think it helps thinking of
you in this way when
no one can correct the
empty in me. Not to say it
won't turn me from god,
instead hold him
accountable. Ask
What the fuck is this?
Seven fucking years.
What the fuck is this?
because I still don't know
where you are buried &
no one is telling me.

Wolves of Saint August

"Listen, once a man kept a wolf in his stomach & the wolf slowly ate him from the inside out"

If I replace the red burden of your name with dogs teeth
then the wolves will never know how I survived. My mouth
is obliged to remind you; prayer becomes an onerous thing; grieving a habit.

Empty pews will never ask your reason remain human to better know
the nature of your punishment. Ask how could you let this happen
to a house of god? There's no need to apologise for my loss. I don't

forgive the dead any longer, come upon us like a judgement
I will invoke your name like the last time church bells rang
Don't argue with me, I'm drunk with skeletons. Your body became

an outbreak of bones & you grew up insisting this hurt was normal. Carved scripture
into a body that fits. The night ends with you
leaving me hypnotised turning skin into epitaphs.

Worshipping dinner party gods *(fugue in D minor)*

Over the kitchen sink, I remove piano remnants
from my mouth. I tried to learn
how to be a bird & its wing bone is in my teeth,
your name brought forth, an empty beer bottle
an isle of violence, the pungent facts
of the bodies jealousy & no knowledge
of sorrow. Making a home
of the tile floor, the revolution has been lying to us again

I could not return to a home
knowing it is unlocked so before I leave,
I proclaim the yearning is reciprocated & kiss it.
Return is the hardest part
so I ensure I don't go. Though I keep pulling
I have not found you
in paper, dead named,
old eyes sellotaped to the sun,
& I'm not one to overthrow
the wounds of my new sanctuary.

The marble effect counter top is now
so convincing in it's oratory, I am a convert
to the minutiae of my own life left unlived.
I pitch my broken mouth to the floor
& wrench the tiles from their position with my teeth
read the guts of home, domestic haruspex.
tenant prophet. I taste grout & footsteps in my bite
making myself comfortable in the insisting
on the primacy of the present
The revolution is an aftertaste.

Over dinner parties I hold the gaze of fortune teller visitors
& insist they open up about their past, there are fishing wires
hooked into my cheek & over the edges
of the table we have stretched out for guests.
From my frenulum a musical theatre staircase collapses
over the okay crockery, & the only slightly bloodied table linen
the ornamental runners stretch down my throat.
& I cannot close my mouth. Any moment now
I know they will pull the tablecloth & disappear my bite.

Mouth stretched lung wide, a chorus
of dancing girls kick their way through my teeth
I know they will ask the question I have been avoiding.
My inability to narrate & absorb the past exhaustively
means I know exactly who will betray me.
I will not ask them to leave, or declare
their love for this house & it's occupants.
Instead invite them into the warm of me.
Acknowledge we both believe ourselves to be right
& accept that we are not.

god Kintsugi II : Ritual of Want &
Ritual of Need

Returning to myself I find
hope is just a prayer to distance,
transience is for those without.
Take me away from it all or bring me closer I beg.

Until my hands: Arbiter of Near Misses;
Culmination of Stories; Saint of Epilogues & All That Jazz,
have felt your hands begging a moment more
remove the holy of leaving

I cannot speak on almosts.
I am complete in this.
I am the last time you will see me
& I bring that with me

The rain, the rain has rejected asylum
says instead to stay & cherish
the satisfaction of home,
ephemera for the bereft

Church of my own abandon.

Gravity as a prescription

The ground's been leaving voicemails for me that it knows I won't listen to. I speak to my mum for the first time in months. She says she bumped into the ground at the supermarket. Noticed it when her card nearly got declined. Said it had been asking after me. Noted we used to be so close & whatever happened to all our promises of forever?

The library has been sending overdue fines for placebos. I've kept them hoping they will start to take effect any second now. I have a habit of over estimating the stated dose. My doctor offers gravity as a prescription. Holds ceilings above my head teasing treatments when I have asked for cures. My doctor withholds a lot of things this way. Mimics the voice of rock bottom so articulately, I swear I look at the infographic & certificate strewn walls to ensure I am not in fact submerged. There is a reassurance in walls like me, that have seen better days.

Still here. They take the time to point out to me I could have something more hideously wrong with me & demands to know if I recognise the signs? I interpret this as a comment on my cowardice & swallow my tongue in case it offers sustenance. They call this a waiting room but it feels more like a being room.

There is a piece of Tuesday embedded wherever my gaze falls. I am sixteen feet tall & five hundred & eighty pounds if I'm a day & I think I am tomorrow most likely. I found ways to open letters I don't want to read. It involves presumption & ridding yourself of any bad news before you hear it. So far it has been quite effective. Tomorrow is avoided & filed away for later.

In a cinema no one can see you cry but they sometimes try to subtitle my grief. I think of the coastline paradox & sandbag the weekend into my jawline. The tide of the doctors office pulls my shoulders into awkward positions. The jetsam of all the bills I haven't paid & answers not given to demands weighs intricately on the infinite of survival. Rock bottom is a byword for *this is the lowest I have been* so far. Perspective is important. The ground is a familiar stressor that I would welcome, were it not for the fact that I have greeted it from so far up this time.

Saint of Spiders

(in a bar at the end of the world after the horsemen have been & gone & there is next to nothing the faithful sidle up to you & sell you their failures as if you haven't already bought it all before)

Have you ever starved yourself? The spider god of empty guts forms a webbing of bile & impatience. They don't believe in him anymore. They say arachnophobia is misplaced in England where even wolf spiders are largely harmless. They say there's a pack mentality in silk & exsanguination. They say the Saint of Spiders is a martyr of the threads. That bluebottles trapped are still worshipping paralysis. That you can predict the future by giving the spiders bodies so they will change it on our behalf. How much do you know of Odontomancy? Of Democracy? Of the ritual of prostate trees not blowing but bowed by the wind? What do you know of guts *guts* $\sqrt{guts}$? Spill yourself out here son, we'll make them predict whatever you want. Here, where they put a levy on the dew caught in morning webs. Here, where apathy only means you don't struggle so as not to draw attention to yourself however trapped you are. Here, where there were ruins once. If the mouths of spiders were made for speaking we would hold them to account & record their testimony. Testimony of their mouths *mouths* $\frac{MOUTHS}{MOUTHS}$. Evidence we could have done better. Evidence of wreckage systems in the holy land. Evidence of crisis actors who attended RADA↓ or whose parents had the funds to send them away to actual disasters or to create them. Now we visit this experiment in the destruction of history & omitted narratives. In the gift shop we purchase merchandise of Hunger. Look at our bellies, aren't they disappearing? Aren't they wonderful absences? Aren't our stomachs an indication of the effort it takes to not believe in anything? Even with all this rhetoric on how everything missing about us is what makes us wonderful, they're still funding bodies. They're still selling us indoctrination as a tourist destination. Saying you *mostly don't feel it when they vomit their enzymes into your bodies to digest you from the outside in.* They say, *they say,* **they say** all these delightful hurtful things. The constitution of the arachnids tells us to be thankful. The propaganda of the wretched; think small that we can control it. Think fast, I want you to look defeat in the face & believe you can abstain from it. Become the awkward wound of a statistic. Anecdotes from emaciated evenings say *give up,* they say *change is not possible* because they benefit from the message being consumed. Survival is a bitter parlance. We call it medicinal & ask if you exonerated yourself & all your glorious infestations. The placebo of a thousand arachnids prevents coughs as they crawl from your lungs & submit an expenditure report for your throat as unavoidable wear & tear.

UNTESTAMENTS
&
APOCRYPHA

Factory made pilgrims

Why do you insist the end isn't worshipped for what it is - an assembly line of hunger arresting its emesis because we are satisfied. I am aware I am a factory born mouth. Gaping need. Worshipping monuments to driftwood because no one can admit we don't know what the fuck we are doing. This uncertainty is all I have left & you will not take this from me. In the peristaltic distance - two hares riot. All of October is against them. Cruel months tempting them to bloodshed before the boredom of hibernation. Bite fever. Anger calenture. Bile Song. Justified homicide. Bloodlust, however mistimed, is a form of desire. They win or lose on sand dunes. You have to admire the lack of compromise in a flight or fuck response like that. If you approach them they will cease fighting & escape. In this way you can call yourself a cunt messiah, one for saving the violent through fear. You can pluck the wild fucking prophet from it's fucking death dance, hold it's feral to your face, teeth bared, quicksand breath smelling of defeat & tell it whatever the fuck it needs to hear but you cannot bring back the spring.

Is That You god? It's Me. A Hornier, More Powerful god.

when he turns
the blood in your water into wine
you will thank him.

when he walks
on the water of your body
you will ask for crueller strides.

when he leaves
the water, rising from the sea to claim you again
you will praise the wickedness of his giving you desire.

torso fugue, the body wants
to leave. It happens sometimes.
you will exalt his name.

abyss language. memento mori
nostalgia. his demand has left
your inhibition mouth

& you still beg for more;
your thorax to abandon you;
to remember death, greeted as a friend.

when he says
he got what he wanted you will thank him
for the mercy of living forever.

international unexploded ordnance day

I've been speed reading self help books again & of course finding bomb disposal guides that read like how not to manuals. You have a way of becoming the type of history that repeats itself. The emptiness inside us both is an amnesty. There is a chance that in the dusty backroads of our youth, I found something that looked like a solution. There is a chance I've been holding out for a disarmament process to exempt the wound we made of each other. There is a chance I tried to take the aching & understand it. The boy's mouth drips nitroglycerine but he thanks heaven he wrapped his fist in tenderness & lust. We try not to read too deep into what this means. The heavens, too, make no discernible effort to translate him.

Where the summer ends, wasteland. Numerous thumbs up to distance. It way. We'll talk about Yellow livers in the hostile nostalgia, wax lyrical of yourself to survive. Seems wistful. There is a chance exclusionary design

but for us, an innocent suns set on the horizon, wasn't supposed to be this having prevented this. architecture of our bodies when you didnt have to eat fitting to spend so long my my body is the preventing me from

remembering. Raising no dispute The boy eats the road, breaking teeth on hot black tarmac, & breathes the phrase *no highly esteemed deed is commemorated here* from glass lungs. & he's right. I remember when all of us were fields, when the feral teeth ridden boys in our history were nightmares only. I remember, we tried to change this but became experts on exploding. In the same way we love one another - humans terraform the ground beneath our feet, to make it fit for whatever inherits the earth from us. I hope it's you. There is a chance everything we ever wrote is only dust waiting to become. The anthropogenic impact of not clearing up after ourselves. There is a chance becoming is all we were meant for. I am learning to live with that

god kintsugi III : How to return the body to its owner

Dear body

We only meet in passing,   this sounds like an ending
Such things are made in earnest   how seeming is such lovely compromise.
My possessions will outlast
my gravid hands   so here's to whatever is holding us.

Bury me with enough coins   to pay the ferryman for a return trip
& spare for those buried without,   bury us with mercy
the generosity of accepting the sound   I chose for me & a secret you can stand to
part with.

Your face will eventually turn to mine   & you will not recognise
from the soil in your ear   how your soul left us
in a reluctant embrace   I want us to wear what we wore
when you told me you first loved me.   I can't
remember what it was   but I hope you do.

of course I am scared   I have waited
exactly as long as you have to meet you
& I want avoid the awkwardness this strangeness pronounces

yours sincerely
the faith in yourself that you needed
            the body rejected   for how it did not fit you

The warm regards of a graveside,   our deepest condolences to ourselves
& a solemn promise   this is not a letter to but from.

Give 'em Hell (a litany for hard times)

If they forbid us from praying
then we must make god experience our bodies
if protest is illegal then we will teach our skin the language of riot
if our hands are taken from us then we pay back in arms.
      if they deny us our voice then we must outgrow our names.

If they tempt the apocalypse
        let us be the horsemen
     If you'll not take the reins, know no heralds are immortal
     if they deny us our living & don't let us die,
     if they extort our healing & claim life's not a right
     if they ration our breath & do not let us speak

if they poison our words & will not let us believe
if they name our enemies to suit their own needs
if their acceptance
     of who we are is conditional
then they only tolerate us
     if intolerance is a virtue
then they will never let us grow
     if we never grow
our mouths will never get the chance

to speak. So tell me what came first. fire or language?

76

if failure, the shrugged shoulder, becomes the world's maxim
the together we must become is a barricade
If you think gods deserve the power of belief
know that belief is bestowed by the believer
& that this world was built for us
& that us is a testament. Us is a promise.

Unrest as renaissance, know the conflict of our bones
Break the social contracts with our bodies
that we will not let be broken
if the old gods will ravage this world we have built,
we will show them they can't take it with them

Give us your wounds & your wounded
better to stand with those who have grown despite & learned
Than those who would deny us our past
We fight like hell for the present.
       to ensure they never have a moment devoid of history
only the future
better the earthquake than the yield.

we will become the water in the cups they deny us
give us this day our daily empty

We will become the flood. [1]

---

[1] give us hope //let us believe // a prayer is a call to arms if done right// & I've not seen a better ccause than this one // I don't believe in anything // except the revolution.

god survivor

heavenly anchor
& the god song
the survival myth,
god-man
breaking
you did not try
remembering
like you said
you would. embrace
the song of the
body of a dead
god child
holy infinite
prohibition god

in the month
of the torso
the most wretched
of virtues
gods heard by
the week of missing
god complainant
in a holy plaintiff.
disputes &
settlements
god found themselves
guilty
of the machine god,
in the survived of it.
god survived by
the fear remaining
in rooms
you left

abandoned
you did not remember
the way the torso
did not succeed
the way the unbelieving
failed failed failed
the infinite

worship of motel rooms &
oil spill saints, wake the
mouth from it's
remembering. To
forfeit. Removing the
awkward from the
machinery, perpetually
forgotten.
that
way you inhale
the weakest of
me
me;
me, in a serrated sainthood
sugared   skin,
sharpened bones
we were all rooting
for you & if we're honest

don't blame yourself
don't believe a word
the holiest child is
a vacant miracle.
in the rooms
without reason

without reason
got lost on the way
without hurting
gave up
the most spectacular
guts claimed asylum
in the limits the body
pronounces

like you promised
consume the tile floor
bathroom from it's
worship of the
not remembering
like you said you
would. Pledge
a violent malfunction

not revealing
awkwardly waiting
in a gambler's body
vices. aposematic,

we're all knives, here
we know the life
we love the razor
for not staying
in the rooms

we could not survive in

October Built Houses

I admit, freely, that I am a place we both used to be.
There are small towns that live & die inside of us
that I believe will serve as compromises to our history
here, in the ruins that October built.

We are two homes-to-have-escaped-from remembering each other.
Haunted by accents we can't shift,
reminding us permanence is for other people
even if we can't help but empathise.

I don't speak for myself when I say
growing up in failures' uniforms makes being found a change.
All we knew was lost.
Is it any surprise our language sounds like missing?
Is it any surprise we speak comfortable silences better than we explain ourselves?

At that part in our friendship where we had to introduce each other
to our former selves, I didn't have it in me to admit -
I knew you didn't like any of who I was.
You stuck with me regardless
& I never thanked you for that

Even if we never talk again our epitaph will read:

"two gluttons for exits survived by distance"

& what a legacy that is to leave behind.
A perpetual longing... .even if it is a longing for quiet.

Sure, we could disinherit the wind together if you want.
Take our bodies full of everyone we used to be,
pretend we want no part of the sky & it's plans for us

but I'm not sure if we should say fuck it so ineoquently
when we have spent so long learning
how to protest being so politely in the first place.

Maybe we're something that needs to have happened, not people to be had.
Maybe we're not questions, it could be we're gods.
Ones that neither of us happen to have faith in
but when I start thinking at these speeds
I want to write a letter to every one I knew who ever believed in me
starting:

Dear whoever,
you were proved right again: I care more about the had than the having
if only because the past tense is so easy to write in.

Perhaps a god without followers is a friend left behind.

I'm in the Autumn of my second chances.
I think redemption gets taken for granted
& forgiveness has a very finite limit.
I think I started with nothing & I still have all of it.

Maybe this doesn't adequately explain anything.
Maybe will this save your mouth the ignominy of saying my name even in passing.
Maybe this shows that even horizons are compromised by endings.
Maybe we'll work better in hindsight.
Maybe the answers as to why don't matter.

I'd like to apologise for having more experience in being left & in leaving than you
& to thank you for staying as long as you did.

god kintsugi IV : Cacophony of Tectonic Shift

Emergency protocols for tenderness willing, I will escape this loss, this blueprint of how to avoid. Herald the momentary collapse of a decade & examine the animal experimentation of time spent at parties. How we'd hang up our dessicated past & point to all the scars that made it easier to escape the cross examination of everyone. & how we, not knowing how not to be defined by a tragedy, would invite loss to talk about how intimately it knows us to the audience of motorways.

How the mood would change in car journeys home. How you would weep, unfold your exhibition skin & try to rewear the artwork you used to be. Tugging at me incessantly & begging me to tell you that no one loved you despite your broken or because of your fixed but because of simply you. & I, wearing my tongue like the road least travelled, would rust a lament & I regret that I could not tell you for certain which it was. & how you would cry yourself to sleep in the back seats of passing traffic. & how I was too focused on the resolution of our carefully orchestrated collapse to properly comfort you & how I would curse myself & my spider tongue once again for failing to strengthen our resolve.

You did yourself a disservice in apologising & have spent too long in being a souvenir, but the piano is asking questions of the hallway again & what were we supposed to have done about it? The god of heights never answers the prayer of descent. So, do we go on talk shows to reminisce our distance? Look lovingly at each other through a warped lens & invite guests called *so far* & *so good* to talk to us about how *It's not how you fall that matters but how you land*? I don't say it lightly, but I would rather die again than have to suffer through another dissection of how we fell apart.

In time, my mouth becomes an excuse. This year has felt like the only time period that held me as close as you did. We will survive this distance like we survived our youth, even if we have to reincarnate as side characters from children's stories that have escaped. With archive footage courtesy of my vacant mouth, I present myself as evidence, corridors twinned with the tendons in my neck & the promise that we will map ourselves in fire exits.

Tenets of faith

1.   LAMENTATIONS

Boys are made from mistakes
made at the expense of others.
Tithes only paid, as pounds of flesh
years too late to be of any use as a cure.

Boys
whose mouths lay derelict for decades, overgrown
with alabaster complications, vows of silence
their only language, faith in themselves
relegated to lost & found boxes.

Boys
as seven years bad luck proof of broken
childhood & shattered homes, reflections
of the penance they endured,
ecclesiastical scars from the shards of
prayers not answered

Boys
born at the exact height they'd eventually be.
who didn't grow to their full reach & so stood, suspended
in air over shoes they would never get to fill. Denied entry to heaven.
Told clerical collars cannot be made of rope.

All trying to be sacred in the shape of the monasteries of men
skin turned slate, tongues tiled to roofs of mouths,
steeples full of bells, warning to stay away.

Held up by expectations. Held up as an example.
Held up by not knowing
collapse is ok sometimes.

2.   ECCLESIASTES

We write blueprints for boys who become
condemned buildings. Who try to unlearn
cathedral centuries of bad habits.

Who are rebuilt as luxury flats,
empty office blocks.
The planned obsolescence of ruin.
We are told that this is progress.

The patron saints & architects of our own demise
trying to become men
who go on pilgrimages to find themselves.
We become studies in shadow
of the father, son & holy ghost
who was never made clear to us.

gods
made from the absence of our role models
or their presence.

Faith invested in preachers
leering from pulpits saying:

> *I didnt want to do this.*

> *You have no idea how sad this makes me.*

> *This is hurting me more than it's hurting you.*

3.   REVELATION

We empty spaces.
Conditioned
to believe no one believes in us.
Raised like the hell we are told we are,

I'd reach through the years of Catholic guilt
if I thought it would change things.
Grab the priest by the throat & say

>   *Father, I cannot be absolved of my sins unless I do better*

& we must do better because we cannot do any worse.

I'd scream this into the empty churches we became
but my tongue, caught in a ritual of words,
would be heard only by a congregation of ghosts.

I have signal fires in my throat. Lighthouse confessionals
that want to sing this admission into shadows.
That old, old hymn of repetitive mistake disorder
sung to the familiar tune of forgive me,
instead of

>   *I will not sin in a way that needs forgiving again*

sung one year after the next.

There is a prayer I tell myself that sounds like a poem.

A prayer that we will learn how to talk.
A prayer addressed to anyone who will listen.
It is a prayer that there will be someone who will.

self compassion in a room full of people who want to sleep with you

Have I told you I loved you today? I bet I haven't. It's hard to sometimes, but I think that I do. I love you like that odd space between a break up & a honeymoon that you call a relationship. I love you like a tooth eager to meet the ground. All it knows of your tongue is what it can discern from the roof over its head. Grateful & cloying. Flossed clean & still smelling of it's old occupants. Yes. That's how I love you. Never easily. But we're learning. You can be both the *missing* & the *here* of it & that both are worthy of love even if not worthy in their own right. We're learning what it means to want to mess up your hair & notice it's gone. To want to massage your psalm & notice the holy is gone. To want to tear up your youth. Every heartache & near miss of it, then notice that too is gone. What's left is metastasized abandon & second chances. What's left is the houses you let collapse. What's left is everything you have built yourself back up from. This ruin, I sense, is the piece you could most do without but still love your stubbornness & brick wall of it. the vodka & twist of it, the last drink & promise of it. How you couldn't bear to let it go & how it *still* defines how you kiss. Yes I love that 14 year old you is still here, all sullen & misunderstood. Do you still keep him around because you are learning how to tell him you love him? It's hard isn't it? But I love that you still love like he needs to be taught. Wearing your history like a ball gag. The fall & the tragedy of it. The violence & attrition of it. The despite & because of it. I love that despite everything you still leave yourself open. Sometimes not learning how to be closed is a good thing Mr I Use Honesty As A Defence, Mr Not Getting Into The Real Of It, Mr They Assume The Worst Must Be Over & Don't Look Any Further Though You Invited Them In. Sometimes being left open is a wound for a reason. But I love that you have almost started caring for yourself, that you almost learned acceptance, that you almost started tidying up as you go. *Almost* is a caveat you pride yourself on isn't it? & I can see why, given the all of it. But do you carry yourself with the grace you give others? Are you as cruel as your thoughts? Are your intentions towards yourself pure? I can see, in this room full of strangers, naked & lusting, & clawing at you, hoping for more of you whilst wrist deep in others. I can see in this forearm & clavicle of it, this broad shoulders & kind eyes of it, that unwilling or unsure of the why of it, you are here. A boy dressed up like a hall of mirrors looking to be loved at an orgy. Where they only want to fuck you & you tell yourself this is close enough. That this will do.

Unrecognisable prayers

O holy list of things I do not need! O commerce! O fear sold as a product, the not having at discount prices! O mighty complicit privilege! O identity theft posing as personality tests! O holy rising moon in my apathy house! Help me decipher this being as an abstract. O apocryphal Holy grail of recognition in anatomical diagrams & grimaced sallow faces! I am a forever vomiting emoji sick of my own callow need to be recognised as being. I am & offer my graven image as a testament to existing. O false idol available in seven affordable monthly payments! These hymns are two way streets, if I open my mouth & contour my virtue signalling *I can make it appear like caring.*

O, holy living as protest! O friends! corroborative scripture I am loved I haven't confessed I wouldn't be here without you, O! My most reverent, intimate calluses from holding on, my apostasy was in never letting you know the scripture of your trust kept my penitence, & O! I have kneeled so as to avoid looking you in the eye. O pantheon of almost! O sermon of us! O most carefully rounded shoulders! O most successful phobia, the high cost of salvation! O Holy companions! I have denied you the ravens who grab sunrise with their claws & swoop upwards pulling the day behind them. They, like you, are miracles.

Things I wish I learned in the undertow

(after Joelle Taylor, Desree, Malaika Kegode & everyone who writes men better than men do but especially after Kim Addonizio)

If you do not know how to touch because you never were softly, if it has been too long since you went to the doctor because you weren't taught how to say I hurt in a language that isn't a weakness, if you are still finding that weakness is a becoming & it does not make you less or if you realise this too late. If no one has ever held you firm & told you *My god, it is good to see you*, & meant it. If you see your friend break in ways you never learned how to & can't think of the first thing to say, or if dialogue was lost under stiff upper lips & fists, if you have no way to tell anyone that you are not the person you see in the mirror or you are & cannot stand to look yourself in the eye, if you are making a habit of making eye contact with traffic, if you do not know how to be fallow, the wasteland of your 9-5 body turned arid from overuse. If you have fled beneath your bed to hide from monsters & found there were more there than when you began. If you build cairns for everyone you used to be. If you can never find the way to say I love you & meant it. If you are learning accountability & accepting your flaws does not entitle you to forgiveness. If you speak to yourself & no one answers. If you are holding on too hard to something that serves no purpose.If you leave now tomorrow you will know how long the day is & how lonely & in the night you will discover just how sharp the angles of absence will be, you will learn via descendants how everyone inherits you, father figure that you could never live up to. Ask how good is your best impression of nothing? Ask if you really know what it means to have to fill a hollow left by all that you were. Ask yourself if you won't sit here for just a moment longer until you decide to be something again.

No I'm not the Messiah, I just work here.

The hours in the evening that makes everything golden & stop hurting, only always.

The inchoate of yearning, & forgetting
that to need is possibly the most human thing to do
& also that mountains do it sometimes.

Eating apples to their core for the sake of orchard stomachs.
The thought of a gift rather than the giving.
& castles erected in backyards to commemorate falling
are not metaphors for anything.

Time as a gift, touch as a language, with punctuation distance, hope as a place,
you as a destination are not allusions to something greater.

The knowledge that telling someone you love them is often the universe
giving you a chance to explain yourself is not a metaphor for anything.

None of these observances, are referring to a larger, better known work
& do not in any way question the divinity of god or self
they just are.
What the speaker is trying to convey is they are not metaphors for something.

No one wants to be a metaphor for something else. Not when nostalgia
is an awkward artist. Not when the benefit of hindsight before the act of happening
is a way of reminding yourself to live in the moment better.

If you thought falling in love was an exercise in joining the search party that is looking
for you, you'll find friends that make it seem nothing like falling but revealing.
Showing someone something beautiful about them, that they had yet to discover.

This is not a metaphor for something, it is a hope.
Something that isn't sacrosanct. How could it be? Our mouths that tell these truths
are not sarcophagi, though we are experts on grieving.

Our tongues are worth more than compassionate leave. I trust it to measure
the grief in our distance so tell me you have missed me & mean it

Tell me you are someone who is all devilled details & boxed gods resisting
introspection. Someone whose hands are boxes unable to cage this.

You & your arrival in other people's lives are not metaphors for anything else.
Who would want to explain away the full of you with a magic trick of phrasing?

Something that proves we are more than figures of speech. We are more
than just a simple method of demonstrating our own finite.

Our tongues were gifted to us by an unruly being who thought it funny
to tattoo a map on our bodies & leave us lost for words.

So if we seem like metaphors trying to explain each other
it must be because we were never given the language to understand

The way I see it, we're all just a narrative trying to prove a point.
The way I see it ultimately we all have some epilogue in mind.
We could all die at any fucking second so I promise - I am getting by in your name.

We are an allegory that helps understand itself by being.

Until we show our hand, full of this magic trick of being that hides in semantics.
I will thank whatever accident caused this exact moment to exist.

The providence of company like yours of friends & of love that I can't explain
This miracle of our existing, this existence I do not deserve.
This fortune of the brightest kind.

god kintsugi V : Being rooms

When dogs stop biting & the hand that feeds becomes a mouth
when food is an escape or a defence
when the restaurant we met in mysteriously burns down
when memories become excuses for not being immortal
when the sun neither rises nor sets on either side,
but stubbornly stays & says the day is where I belong.

When your ribs are less a cage & more an exhibit
when tomorrow holds possibility to ransom
when your touch is too late
when the taxonomies of leaving & of hurting become apparent
when you say I didn't want the world to end & mean it.
when I reconcile to remain an afterthought & never an epitaph.
when the porcelain jaw of a moment breaks, from not speaking,

I will weep & nod & acknowledge that I too, have found no respite in god.
I will reject gravity's pious message just this once.
I will mouth the mornings we couldn't afford,
talk long in this daily sadness that English is.
This strange medicine.
This stubborn rhetoric.
I will hang my head. Bury my hands in unmarked graves
& grieve that I will never touch you again.

30 silvers will stand you a bottle or a goodbye in this Nowhere Town

When your expertise is being held captive,
open windows do not care for height.

Grievances distill this day into the next,
tying the sunset into a noose.
I believe night to be most holy.

I was never ground floor.
The important thing
about falling is other people
will always try
to catch you until they can't.

If   you   feel   like   this   is   your   fault   then   it   is.

I know how to consumate
a lie, I know how to go down
a poor lover.

whilst falling I was a missing person poster
telling me I wasn't
here anymore.

I gave the game away by loving
the morning more than the night

*Amen**

*One day you will realise you love yourself & even that will surprise you. To want not to hate the chalk outline of a face that appears in mirrors when you aren't home. For sobriety say charity - it's a kindness to everyone to not poison yourself. Here it is Autumn always, you had to learn the long way having been mistaken for the letting go of any old wound but you did learn. You ran away from yourself & everything you were but look how far you have come. It is easy to forget how nostalgia is contagious - hard to commit to not destroying yourself or honouring your former lives by acknowledging the tragedy they were but you will make it - you must.

Leviathan *(/lɪˈvaɪ. əθən/; לִוְיָתָן, Līvəyāṯān)*

THE MOURNABLE BODY OF THE LAST DAYS IS COMING Dear wreckage, do you still love me? My body is committed to something it was not ready for. Keep the wound from its waking. Wreckage, I am only temporary. I rupture a fresh mouth of desolate mountain range knuckles. Every backwater that's escaped from leaves bodies in its wake - rich soup of the dead. We that come from dying towns have seen the end times & they are man made & we are powerless. We have seen the phantom of peace & we are haunted. My body is a city that abandoned its populace. Every realisation evicts a fresh narrative - inheritance of spines. How does it end? Wreckage, Leviathan, Flooder, Becomer. Tell me. Tell me there's reasoning in rationing my breathing. Wreckage, churn the gravedirt - Tell me you still love me. I've a loathing of conspiracies in my insect wings. Flooder I am building the body of an iceberg. Leviathan - I am building a shipwreck to carry us. Becomer - I can learn not to breathe if I have to.

PARAMEDICS STAND AWKWARD AT THE ACCIDENT REHEARSAL PROUDLY PHOTOGRAPHING THEIR IMPENDING DISASTERS & the road never stops. Not once. Not even for breathing. You keep your hand gripped tight against the bone of the wheel & watch the landscape disappear bedside you. The flashing neon of all the holy mountains & the wreckage & the icebergs & the roadside attraction of all the graveyards raised in your name & you stop to buy cigarettes; Mortuary Opening Day memorabilia; yesterday's gas station sushi. Useless souvenirs just to feel something. Anything & you drive three more days on collectors' edition's bucketfuls of vomit. Eight hundred more miles of holy scenery, reliquary of grieving. Till you remember you don't drive & the things you have been finding in your bile in the sink are all too familiar; crime scene revelation; empire of sharks; priest of guillotines semen; whale oil; a pocket empty of teeth; your last text left on read; the hands of empty throated boys & all of your claims to immortality. Till you find our father who art of knives; whose blades made purpose in both of our skin; whose living body is sharpened & redeemed by coarse marble. Till he asks: was our redemption worth the world? Tell me Apocalypse songs. Leviathan. The gentrification of our history has been vetoed by the council of names. Leviathan. We'll do one better & call this body distance, distance from each time we tried & failed & how despite all the fevered hallucinations of sainthood you know the mountains will never stop. How even in your reflection the scenery is still peeling away behind you, the skin of the horizon burnt fresh anew, & we keep going & keep going & we keep going & the road never stops not once, not even for breathing.

MISE EN ABYME of falling asleep on fire & before that of a flat cold for 6 months warmed by the mutually assured destruction of promising yourself to someone you couldn't be & before that a house turned ruin, & before that the bodies of all the most beautiful, tattooed boys drinking our dying & closing doors with the weight of our corpses. & before that a place to dismantle one's history & before that there's all these people that want to survive. & before that all the touch starved are begging to be fearless. & before that addicts are people haunted by visions of their past lives who have the benefit of having been there for real. I want to stop being mistaken for the messiah. I promise, I'm just someone who lived again by accident & didnt stop.

EPILOGUE AS EXCUSE What if we get to the end & find all our good work was for nothing?

APPLAUDING AMBULANCE CHASERS FOR THEIR EMPATHY & an addict asks since I have seen the face of god how do I do normal? How do I go back to being without? & god is not stopping calling like he hasn't got the message; & god is horrified we could find holy in anything but him; & god has tried to find ways to get messages to me through other means like appearing as abusive partners to people I love or setting himself on fire so I can't help but notice him. He transforms bodies. But a miracle is a heinous thing. The way your father does it, I don't want to believe, Leviathan. How can I do better when all I know is need & want & leaving? Pilgrim, if I turn myself back around & end where I began, is it still a pilgrimage? Leviathan. Has all this meant anything to anyone? The loneliest whale calls back to something it thinks it heard & when I say my name is Sam & I am an alcoholic the voice echoing back is me. Only me running down the hallway of throwing knives - At night, the day becomes a door which no one closes then the ground eats you & you are grateful. Wake the body from its houses. The time has come to stop dying. Rhinos tried to attack the butterflies that came to lap at their tears & I made a lot of plans to relapse today but none of them came to fruition. The problem is sober isn't a happy ever after, it's the start.

BIBLIOGRAPHY, NOTES & REFERENCES

Behemoth uses words from the book of Job. J. Green, G. Rickly, D. Kensrue & C. Voltato amongst others wrote extensively on the revelations following RTAs & as such is considered in this canon. The phrase the exhibition of being human is a nod to Daniel Borzutzky.

god fragment i: Jehovah's Wetness the title is taken from the Sly & The Family Drone song of the same name from their album *Gentle Persuaders* (2019 love love records)

Paranoia Theology uses words from China Mieville's book: *Kraken* (2010 Macmillan)

Requiem for Open & Abandoned Spaces references *The Navidson Record*, a documentary exploring impossible architecture. Takes its form from Mozart's Requiem.

This is how angels make themselves known The phrase "*I wouldn't miss me either*" is directly lifted from Quantice Never Crashed's song "Two bullets & a gun"

† **Allographacy** - the practice of ritual divination by organ donation. Putting other animals entrails into sacrifices to provide more favourable extispicy † **See Saint Eulalia**

Cupio Dissolvi inspired by the phrase found on German composer Stefan Wolpe's Headstone; "When I die one thousand birds will fly from my mouth". James Munoz references children swallowed by telephones in "*Get Up You Son Of A Bitch, Cause Mickey Loves Ya*"

Cupio Dissolvi, How to Turn An Injury Into A Cult & How to find the body were all published in Sticky Fingers Publishing FDBNHLLLTTFBELONGING

god fragment IV: Piano Tuner of Earthquakestakes its name from the Brothers Quay film. Concepts explored in the poem have been quoted in the essay "The disappearing of new humanity" which appeared in issue 151 of New Mendacium Magazine (2018, Liar Press) The piano-exploding-through-skin sequence originally included in the preamble to this poem was removed by the BBFC for *gratuitous medical detail of a metaphorical injury* we acquiesced their editing in order to ensure we would achieve an ⑱ certificate for this book & avoid censorship.

Weakerthan - takes its form from the Weakerthans song *Elegy for Gump Wolsley*

Netflix & Chill Only Make It Existential was published in Cipher Press's *There Will Always be Nights Like This*.

Hellbent takes words from the Rite of Exorcism & its form from Big Thief's song; *Not*

To Praise Prosthesis takes its title from an Orchid Song & subtitle from *Sabina Spielrein's essay - Journal Of Analytical Psychology 1920*

god Kintsugi I: Fifty Shades of Grace The phrase *body festival* can be read as *the airing of grievances* or *funeral for a friend* depending on your point of view. The poem is indebted to the Philosophy of Roberta Sparrow.

Patron Saint of Second chances an early version was published by anti-heroin chic mag

REDEEMER uses words from Bishop Fenelon's Prayer to Do God's Will.

The unique grief of the apostle of bones, I should point out the reason I was isolated in grieving a friend is entirely due to my own destructive behaviour & past actions. This piece is not a condemnation of anyone's grieving process but my own.

Wolves of Saint August uses words from Mike Mignola's Hellboy comics & the title is lifted directly from a Hellboy story of the same name.

Worshipping dinner party gods the phrase "primacy of the present" is taken from the essay *What's Next is the Past* by Lucas Grant
https://www.tandfonline.com/doi/full/10.1080/08989575.2019.1542845

Saint of Spiders ↓ You know the "pristine" ones who somehow made it through 15 arduous years of always getting the part they auditioned for after an expensive drama school, private tutoring, knowing the right people, having money bless the palms & privilege break the rungs of their contemporaries who only lived whilst making art. The ones who eventually somehow get a part in lauded period dramas of popular remakes of existing art by minority artists to eventually be invited on Newsnight, & OK magazine & The Daily Mail & GMTV following numerous cancellations to tell the concerned reporter of their struggle whilst repeating the government line to sympathetic & pliant audiences that there is no war in Ba Sing Se & who wins awards for the cinematography of their propaganda.

International Unexploded Ordinance Day is a genuine day. The format is an homage to Adrian B Earle's boyshapedspace from his pamphlet *5000hurts* (2019, Burning Eye Books)

†**Undertow** the phrase used throughout is indebted to Honey Baxter

Gravity as a Prescription title was provided by Emily Harrison. In fact any longer titles in this work are equally indebted to Emily Harrison & Fall Out Boy. The phrase *I am sixteen feet tall & five hundred & eighty pounds* is an homage to David Wojnarowicz's *Close to the Knives, A Memoir of Disintegration* (Canongate books, 1992)

god kintsugi IV : Cacophony of Tectonic Shift the phrase *so far so good* & *it's not the falling it's how you land* are both translations of the central theme taken from the 1995 Movie La Haine. This poem takes concept of motorway white noise as a form of auxiliary language from the studies & field recordings of Dr Elias Worthy 1963 - 1994

self compassion in a room full of people who want to sleep with you was written after two prompts from Josie Alford.

No, I'm not the messiah I just work here was written after David Ralph Lewis' prompt "fortune of the brightest kind" for Bristol Tonic

Leviathan: the phrase Mise En Abyme is a cinematic & artistic technique whereby the subject holds an image of itself holding an image of itself. It is often used to denote foreshadowing

NOTES: the poems **"vanishing point"**, **"a man lies dead…"**, **"apostle of bones"** & **"god survivor"** are all contrapuntal forms known as Corinthians. They are intended to be read as you see fit. A sixth heavily disputed god fragment is rumoured to exist. Scholars postulate that it's lack of inclusion in this text means this must be considered incomplete. Further work relating to errant Saints can be found on the Beheading. release: *Evisceration Songs* (outsider art 2021) & in Issues of Riggwelter. The Bible 2 is also an album by AJJ - this work is unrelated but you should still check out the album, it's very good. Any likenesses to characters real or imaginary is considered metaphorical. If you find yourself in the book, seek medical help immediately or theological intervention at the very least. This book neither predicts nor condones the apocalypse & is not affiliated with any heralds of the end times My publishers have advised me to note for the avoidance of any doubt I am not the messiah nor are we affiliated in any way.

THANKS as mentioned in the dedication this book would not have been possible without the endless patience of Myriam San Marco who helped shape the first draft of this book into its accepted form. Honourable nods to my Gender Agnostic Gospel Choir of Honey Baxter, Pascal Vine & Jonathan Kinsman whose edits, late night last minute "please look at this poem for me & tell me it's not shit" confidence boosts have got me through the process of being a poet. An endless debt of gratitude to my Milk family; Malaika, Beth & Tom & to Danny & the Raise the Bar family both of whom gave me guidance & purpose & support during my formative years of navigating the poetry world & let me see endless amounts of really cool poets for free. Terry Pratchett & Neil Gaiman opened worlds in my head & I've never found a way to close them off nor wanted to. Thanks to the Evil Dead for existing. I won't be able to name every poet that inspired me with the appellations & praise they deserve but thanks to Ciaran Hodgers, Nafeesa Hamid, Emily Harrison, Jasmine Gardosi, Josie Alford, Joelle Taylor, Czesław Miłosz, Cal Wensley, Safiya Kamaria Kinshasa, 1990s Chris, Desrée, Scarlett Ward, Richard Siken, Vanessa Kisuule, Chris Beale, Tom Sastry, Danez Smith, Jeremy Toombs, Aiysha Humphries,Taran Spalding Jenkin, Dan Smith of Listener, Sam Sax, Travis Alablanza, John K. Samson, Saili Katebe, Michael Lee, Daniel Borzutzky, Salena Godden, Sarah Macready, Kat Lyons, Stefan Mohamed, Johannes Göransson, Caroline Teague, Shagufta Iqbal, Helen Sheppard, Leon Preistnall, Jay Bernard, Melanie Branton, Fran Lock, Roger Robinson, Jess May Davies, Ilya Kaminski, Kathryn O Driscoll, Eve Piper, Shivanee Ramlochan, Sophie Sparham, Hanif Willis Abdurraqib, Caroline Bird, Melissa Lee Houghton, Jake Wild Hall, The Repeat Beat Poet, Rebecca Tantony, Celia Knapp, Bohdan Piaseki, & that strange boy who wore doc martens & yelled about the sun & the universe imploding who I saw once at Milk whilst it was still at the Halo who I have not stopped thinking about since & genuinely any of y'all who I have caught at open mics or online or wherever & have made me write better.

Massive thanks to Stuart at Verve for taking this weird book into your welcoming arms. I owe you so much. With thanks as well to Amy Acre, Bridget Hart & Adrian B Earle who have edited poems in this collection at various stages.

Big love to my Bristol Punk family you beautiful goth weirdos I love each & every one of you.

Finally, Infinite Thanks to The Endless; the real ones who have known me through it all & still like me kinda, this one is a decade long dedication to you & I appreciate it.

ABOUT VERVE POETRY PRESS

Verve Poetry Press is a quite new and already award-winning press that focused initially on meeting a local need in Birmingham - a need for the vibrant poetry scene here in Brum to find a way to present itself to the poetry world via publication. Co-founded by Stuart Bartholomew and Amerah Saleh, it now publishes poets from all corners of the UK - poets that speak to the city's varied and energetic qualities and will contribute to its many poetic stories.

Added to this is a colourful pamphlet series, many featuring poets who have performed at our sister festival - and a poetry show series which captures the magic of longer poetry performance pieces by festival alumni such as Polarbear, Matt Abbott and Genevieve Carver.

The press has been voted Most Innovative Publisher at the Saboteur Awards, and has won the Publisher's Award for Poetry Pamphlets at the Michael Marks Awards.

Like the festival, we strive to think about poetry in inclusive ways and embrace the multiplicity of approaches towards this glorious art.

www.vervepoetrypress.com
@VervePoetryPres
mail@vervepoetrypress.com